MENSA

MIGHTY MIND BENDERS

NEW WORD PUZZLES

Carolyn Skitt

CARLTON

CAN YOU JOIN MENSA?

Solving puzzles can be a rewarding experience. The moment when you discover you have unravelled the puzzle compiler's convoluted logic always brings a glow of satisfaction. But we thought you deserved something more. So Mensa are offering tangible proof of your mental prowess. Solve the following fiendish puzzles and we will send you a free certificate as proof of your achievement.

Puzzle 1

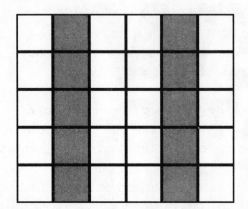

Rearrange the order of the following words and place one on each line of the grid above. If placed in the correct order, a flower name will appear in each of the shaded columns. What are the two flowers?

Sprays   **Floppy**
Cuckoo   **Biceps**
Stripe

Puzzle 2

I am a fruit.
Change one letter and I am found on the coast.
Change another letter and I am a communal seat.
Change another letter and I am a bundle.
Change one final letter and I am a meal.
What was I and what did I become?

Puzzle 4

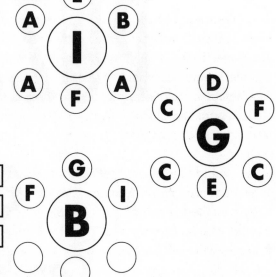

What letters are missing from the last three circles?

Puzzle 3

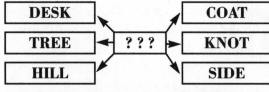

Which three-letter word can be attached to the end of the words to the left, and to the front of the words to the right, to give six longer words?

• •

There, you did it! Now write the answers on a postcard, together with your name and address, and send them to Mensa Puzzle Challenge (Words), Mensa House, Freepost, Wolverhampton, WV2 1BR (no stamp needed). If your answers are correct we will send you a certificate and details of how to join Mensa.

MENSA

MIGHTY MIND BENDERS

NEW
WORD
PUZZLES

If you have enjoyed the puzzles in this book why not try another title in the Mensa series?

Mensa New Number Puzzles
Mensa Logic Puzzles
Mensa Improve Your Mind Power
Mensa Family Quiz Book

THIS IS A CARLTON BOOK

Text copyright © British Mensa Limited 1997
Design and artwork copyright © Carlton Books Limited 1997

This edition published by Carlton Books Limited 1997

A CIP catalogue for this book is available from the British Library

ISBN 1-85868-249-5

Printed and bound in Italy

INTRODUCTION

The world's fascination with word puzzles is almost as old as civilization. Riddles that everyone knows today, like the old chestnut, "As I was going to St. Ives I met a man with seven wives... ", have exact equivalents in the Babylonia of Biblical times. Today, when so many traditional pastimes seem to have been superseded by more exciting games spiced with modern technology, word puzzles are more popular than ever.

Mensa's puzzle books have in many ways become victims of their own success. Our early efforts sold so widely that now each new book has to be written with an eye to foreign markets. We not only have to cope with the differences between British and American English, but with the need for the books to be readily translatable into a wide variety of other languages. We are proud to have editions not only in French and German but in less widely spoken languages such as Finnish and Afrikaans.

Working under such constraints has pushed us to heights of ingenuity and creativity which we little dreamt of when the series began. This book is the work of my colleagues Carolyn Skitt and Bobby Raikhy. Carolyn is the powerhouse of Mensa's puzzle writing department. Her work appears in countless newspapers and magazines. Though you may not recognize her name you will probably have tried her puzzles before. And Bobby is responsible for the technical side, getting Carolyn's ideas onto the computer. As usual, puzzles have been checked by the ever-keen David Ballheimer, whose enthusiasm knows no bounds.

This international outlook exactly matches the world view of Mensa itself. We have well over 100,000 members in countries throughout the world. They enjoy a social club that is unique. There is only one criterion for entering Mensa and that is the ability to pass an intelligence test within the top two percent. The members meet for social and intellectual stimulation and soon find themselves part of a true "intelligence network" which spans the globe. What is more, with the advent of the internet, they find contact with other Mensans throughout the world has never been easier.

If you would like to join Mensa contact us at: British Mensa Limited, Mensa House, St John's Square, Wolverhampton, WV2 4AH England, (tel 01902 772771). American Mensa Limited is at 2626 E 14th Street, Brooklyn, New York 11235-3992, USA, or contact Mensa International, 15 The Ivories, 628 Northampton Street, London N1 2NY, England who will be happy to put you in touch with your own national Mensa.

R. P. Allen

Robert Allen
Editorial Director
Mensa Publications

Can you work out what letter needs to be inserted in the middle to form four dances by combining opposite segments?

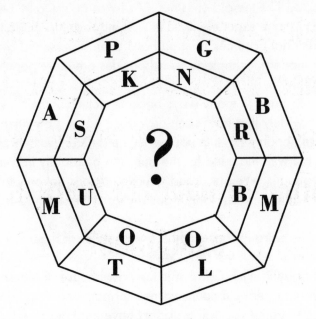

SEE ANSWER 122

PUZZLE 2

Move from square to touching square – including diagonals – to discover the name of a city.

P	H	N	G
C	E	A	G
P	O	E	N

SEE ANSWER 9

At an exhibition there are 207 Calvin Klein creations, 512 outfits by Vivienne Westwood and 100 Jasper Conran outfits. How many items by Giorgio Armani are there at the exhibition?

SEE ANSWER 17

PUZZLE 4

The names of the following ten chefs can be found in this grid on either vertical, horizontal or diagonal lines. Can you find them?

Raymond Blanc

Paul Bocuse

Robert Carrier

Keith Floyd

Rosamund Grant

Ken Hom

Bruno Loubet

Gary Rhodes

Albert Roux

Anthony Tobin

T	N	A	R	G	D	N	U	M	A	S	O	R
B	Y	N	L	K	L	Q	O	X	C	B	O	A
Q	W	T	F	Z	P	H	K	U	J	B	G	Y
Y	G	H	V	S	N	X	E	O	E	R	C	M
D	V	O	W	E	M	D	I	R	S	U	K	O
J	K	N	K	D	B	P	T	T	U	N	O	N
P	M	Y	S	O	S	C	H	R	C	O	P	D
P	F	T	Y	H	A	Y	F	E	O	L	J	B
Z	W	O	U	R	Z	G	L	B	B	O	C	L
F	C	B	R	Y	Q	K	O	L	L	U	F	A
Y	V	I	D	R	J	F	Y	A	U	B	R	N
W	E	N	V	A	Y	Q	D	P	A	E	W	C
R	G	K	P	G	R	Z	B	Y	P	T	P	Q

SEE ANSWER 27

By taking a segment and finding its pair the names of four books
from the Old Testament can be made. What are they?

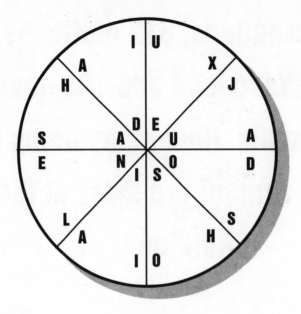

SEE ANSWER 37

In the china department of a large store there are 90 items of Wedgewood, 120 items of Royal Doulton and 140 items of Royal Worcester. How many items of Spode are there?

SEE ANSWER 43

The vowels have been missed out of the following groups of letters.
Replace the vowels and rearrange each group to form the
name of a city. What are the four cities?

STPDB

DNNL

KHLCSTM

RMDD

SEE ANSWER 52

The family names of three athletes have been merged together here.
Who are they?

K	N	E	L	S	L
N					E
H		G	B		O
C			J		L
N	O	A	U		Y
					N

SEE ANSWER 61

Rearrange each of the following groups of letters to form a place in the United States. Which is the odd one out?

AILFORD
ALEEWARD
ORKNYBOL
OZARNIA

SEE ANSWER 58

PUZZLE 10

If the code for Monica Seles is  **GIHCWU MYFYM** who are these other famous tennis stars?

(i) **JUN WUMB**

(ii) **MNYZZC ALUZ**

(iii) **UHXLY UAUMMC**

(iv) **GULNCHU HUPLUNCFIPU**

(v) **WIHWBCNU GULNCHYT**

SEE ANSWER 66

2B	5D	4A		3A	1D	1B	4E	5E	1A
			▓						
1E	3E	2E		2C	5B	4C	3B	1C	2D

The word frame above, when filled with the correct letters, will give the name of a pop singer. The letters are arranged in the coded square below. There are two possible alternatives to fill each square of the word frame, one correct, the other incorrect. Who is the singer?

	A	B	C	D	E
1	Y	R	V	N	B
2	P	F	M	Q	G
3	J	L	Y	W	O
4	B	U	K	C	S
5	D	A	T	H	E

SEE ANSWER 75

Two letters are missing from each of the following anagrams of famous people. Can you spot what letters are missing (maybe more than once) and how the people are connected?

TWE - - -   YGU - -   DESI - -   TGRE - - -

SEE ANSWER 81

In a car race six cars are lined up behind each other. No. 12 is two places in front of No. 3 who is two places in front of No. 21. No. 7 is behind both No. 11 and No. 3 but in front of No. 21. No. 8 is in front of No. 21 but behind No. 11. What is the finishing order of the cars if car No. 21 moves forward two positions, car No. 8 moves back 3 places, car No. 3 moves forward two places, car No. 11 moves back two places and car No. 12 moves forward one place?

SEE ANSWER 93

PUZZLE 14

Can you work out what letter needs to be inserted in the middle to form four famous composers by combining opposite segments?

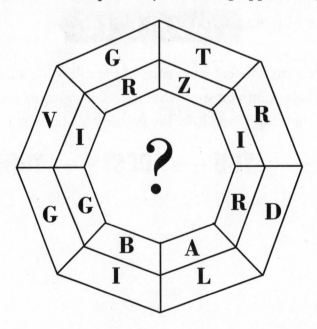

SEE ANSWER 119

What is the next letter in this sequence?

C H L O ?

SEE ANSWER 84

PUZZLE 16

*Adam drinks Advocaat
and he drives a Datsun.
He has a collection of albums
by Annie Lennox.
Does Adam fly with Virgin
or Monarch airline?*

SEE ANSWER 98

Four connected names are concealed here. What are they?

WEISSHORN
CHINA
CHANEL
TANGANYKA

SEE ANSWER 108

Rearrange these four American states in the grid provided so that a European currency can be read down the shaded boxes:

Arkansas, Maryland, Illinois and Michigan.

What is the currency?

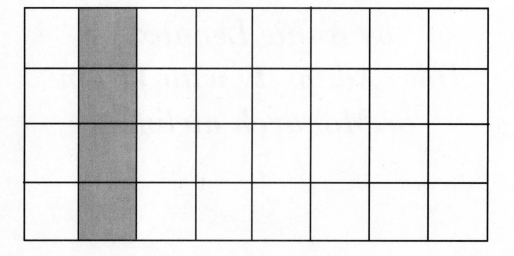

SEE ANSWER 110

Complete the square with the letters of P A R I S. When completed no row, column or diagonal line will contain the same letter more than once. One horizontal line will spell the word correctly. What letter should replace the question mark?

P	A	R		
				?
		S	P	

SEE ANSWER 126

PUZZLE 20

Collect one letter from each segment to give the name of an American state. What is it?

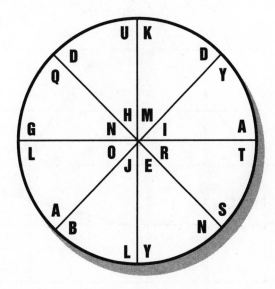

SEE ANSWER 134

What letter is missing from the end turret?
Clue: Actors

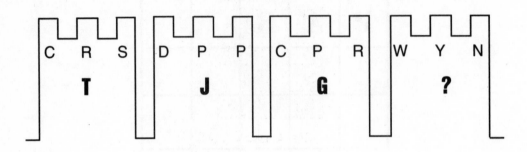

C R S D P P C P R W Y N
T   J   G   ?

SEE ANSWER 140

Two sides of this pyramid can be seen, but the other two are obscured. Two eight-letter country names are written round the pyramid. What are they?

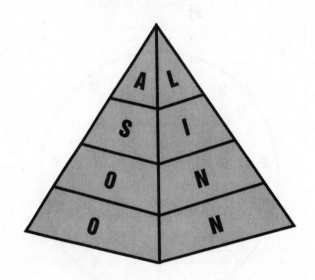

SEE ANSWER 145

PUZZLE 23

A knight, which moves either one square horizontally and two vertically or two horizontally and one vertically, is positioned on this unusual chess board on position A1. Move to each square once in the correct sequence to find the names of four famous scientists.

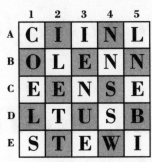

	1	2	3	4	5
A	C	I	I	N	L
B	O	L	E	N	N
C	E	E	N	S	E
D	L	T	U	S	B
E	S	T	E	W	I

SEE ANSWER 150

PUZZLE 24

This is an unusual maze. Find four separate routes through the maze without any route crossing another, although they may share the same path. On each route collect 7 letters only to give you the names of four books in the Old Testament.

SEE ANSWER 156

In a horse race Sawgrass came second and Sea Dancer came fourth.

Where did Sky Trap and Noble Romance finish?

SEE ANSWER 162

PUZZLE 26

Some letters have been omitted from this alphabet.
Use the missing letters to form the name of a car manufacturer.

W K C Y D Z I B H
G X P F
M O J S V Q

SEE ANSWER 2

Move from square to touching square – including diagonals – to discover the name of a composer.

H	C	T	S
I	A	V	K
K	O	Y	Z

SEE ANSWER 10

At a garage there are 5 Rovers, 115 Vauxhalls and 50 Renaults. How many Suzukis are there?

SEE ANSWER 18

The vowels have been missed out of the following groups of letters. Replace the vowels and rearrange each group to form the name of an American state. What are the four states?

SYNPLVNN

SSMTSTSCH

CTTCCNN

NMNTS

SEE ANSWER 53

The names of the following ten champagnes can be found in this grid on vertical, horizontal and diagonal lines. Can you find them?

Ayala
Bollinger
De Venoge
Deutz
Gosset
Henriot
Lanson
Pol Roger
Ruinart
Salon

D	G	J	B	F	H	C	L	G	B
D	E	U	T	Z	E	A	A	O	M
C	T	V	H	W	N	P	L	S	F
P	R	V	E	S	R	L	A	S	H
S	A	L	O	N	I	Q	Y	E	K
K	N	N	J	N	O	X	A	T	D
B	I	W	G	V	T	G	Q	B	W
D	U	E	Z	K	F	X	E	Y	G
F	R	E	G	O	R	L	O	P	Y
Q	G	X	V	C	H	X	Z	O	D

SEE ANSWER 28

By taking a segment and finding its pair the names of four tennis stars can be found. Who are they?

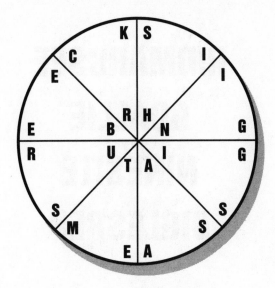

SEE ANSWER 38

PUZZLE 32

Certain pop stars are going on tour over the next few months. Meat Loaf has 6 gigs arranged, Gloria Estefan has 14 gigs organized and George Michael has 12 gigs arranged. How many Bon Jovi gigs will there be?

SEE ANSWER 44

Rearrange each of the following groups of letters to read the names of four famous people. Which name is the odd one out?

HIDMARCSEE

GOALLIE

NINESITE

BIGLESREP

SEE ANSWER 59

These anagrams of famous pop stars surnames have had two letters removed from them. Can you name the stars and what letters have been removed (maybe more than once)?

LLCIS – –

EL – – – –

SEJ – –

DDMAI – –

KACJS – –

SEE ANSWER 82

The names of three film stars have been merged together here.
Who are they?

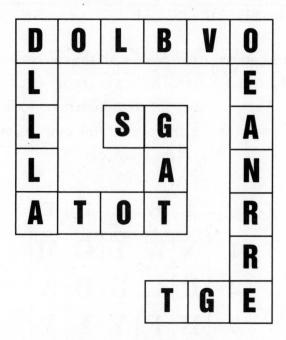

SEE ANSWER 62

If the name WOODROW WILSON is

⊘ ⊕ ⊖ ⊘ ⊘ ⊖ ⊕ ⊗   ⊘ ⊘ ⊘ ⊘ ⊖ ⊖

Who are the other U.S. Presidents?

SEE ANSWER 67

23

1E	4A	3C	3A	1D	5C	3D		4D	1D	4C	1A	4E
5C	1C	2B	2D	4B	2E	5B		1A	5E	2E	3B	2C

The word frame above, when filled with the correct letters, will give the name of a tennis player. The letters are arranged in the coded square below. There are two possible alternatives to fill each square of the word frame, one correct, the other incorrect.

Who is the tennis player?

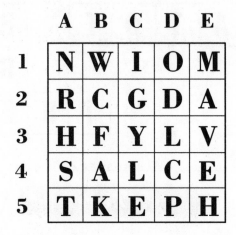

	A	B	C	D	E
1	N	W	I	O	M
2	R	C	G	D	A
3	H	F	Y	L	V
4	S	A	L	C	E
5	T	K	E	P	H

SEE ANSWER 76

What are the next two letters in this sequence?

B D G I M O ? ?

SEE ANSWER 85

*Looking at one side of a bus with two rows of single
seats you can see four seats upstairs and four downstairs.
Mrs Davis is sitting two seats behind Mr Evans.
Mrs Graves is sitting above Mrs Bates
and Mr Adams is sitting above Mr Connors.
Mr Evans sits above Mrs Harris at the front of the bus.
Mr Connors is sitting three seats behind Mrs Harris.
Mrs Davis sits on the top deck and Mr Francis
sits behind Mrs Bates on the lower deck.
Who is sitting where?*

SEE ANSWER 94

PUZZLE 40

Laura wears Chanel clothes and her perfume is Oscar de la Renta. Her favourite sculptor is Jules Dalou and she likes Royal Worcester for her dinner service. Is Laura's favourite tennis player Martina Navratilova or Steffi Graf?

SEE ANSWER 99

If the name of a book from the Old Testament is placed with each of the following groups of letters, each group can be rearranged to give the name of a pop singer or pop group. Who are they?

(i) HNONNN
(ii) VONI
(iii) LONIYET

SEE ANSWER 109

Rearrange the order of these six famous actors' second names to give the name of another famous actor in the shaded diagonal line.

Steve MARTIN, Andy GARCIA, Gary COOPER, Eddie MURPHY, Keanu REAVES, Lee MARVIN.

Who is the actor given in the diagonal?

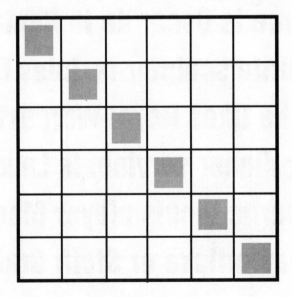

SEE ANSWER 111

PUZZLE 43

Can you work out what letter needs to be inserted in the middle to form four capital cities by combining opposite segments?

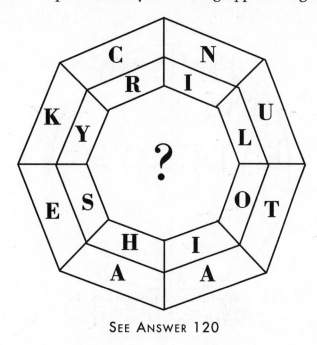

SEE ANSWER 120

PUZZLE 44

Complete the square with the letters of I D A H O. When completed no row, column or diagonal line will contain the same letter more than once. One horizontal line will spell the word correctly. What letter should replace the question mark?

?				
	A	H	O	
		O	I	

SEE ANSWER 127

Take one letter from each segment to find
the name of a Canadian city. What is it?

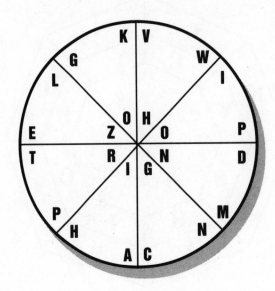

SEE ANSWER 135

PUZZLE 46

What letters are missing from the end boxes?

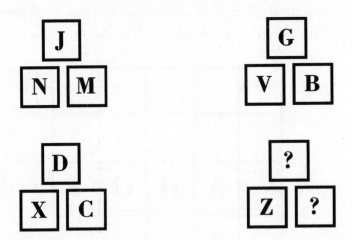

Two sides of this pyramid, on a triangular base, can be seen the other one is obscured. Two six-letter composers' names are written round the figure. Who are they?

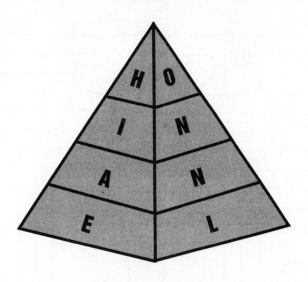

SEE ANSWER 146

PUZZLE 48

A knight, which moves either one square horizontally and two vertically or two horizontally and one vertically, starts at the shaded square of this small chess board visiting each square without returning to the same square twice. Find the route which spells out four famous cartoon characters.

I	R	P	I	O
B	C	G	E	A
E	L		Y	B
I	A	T	L	D
U	L	N	M	O

SEE ANSWER 151

The maze below contains four names of actors and actresses. Find four separate routes through the maze without any route crossing another, although they may merge. On each route collect six letters only to give you the names of the four actors and actresses.

FINISH

START

SEE ANSWER 157

In a car race the Audi was 3 places ahead
of the Mercedes. The Ferrari was 2 places ahead
of the Renault and the Ligier was somewhere
between the Mercedes and Ferrari.

In what position was the Ligier if
none of the cars were level and
there were only five cars?

SEE ANSWER 163

PUZZLE 51

Complete the square using the letters of P S A L M. When
completed no row, column or diagonal line will contain the same
letter more than once. One horizontal line will spell the word
correctly. What letter should replace the question mark?

			P	
		S		
	A	L		
	M			
				?

SEE ANSWER 130

Take one letter from each segment to find the
name of a city in the USA. What is it?

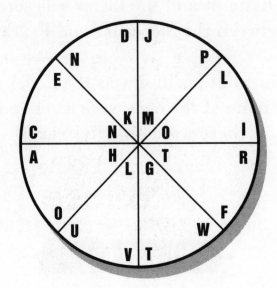

SEE ANSWER 138

PUZZLE 53

The letters surrounding each triangle are the consonants of a
famous sports person's name. The letters inside the triangle have a
connection with each person. What letter should replace the
question mark in the fourth triangle?

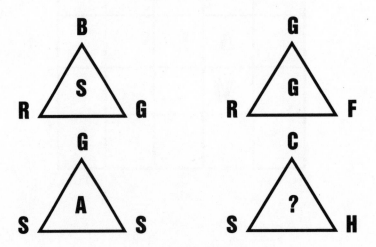

SEE ANSWER 144

Two sides of this pyramid can be seen, but the other two are obscured. Two eight-letter former American presidents are written around the pyramid. Who are they?

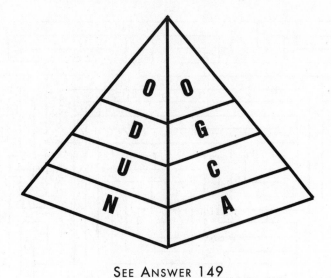

SEE ANSWER 149

A knight, which moves either one square horizontally and two vertically or two horizontally and one vertically, starts at the shaded square of this small chessboard visiting each square without returning to the same square twice. Find the route which spells out six names of people which are also books in the Bible.

L	N	H	A	R	D
U	I	E	A	S	S
I	E	O	A	H	E
J	A	E	A	I	D
S	S	X	U	H	M
E	L	T	U	O	S

SEE ANSWER 154

This is an unusual maze. Find four separate routes through it without any route crossing another, although they may merge. On each route collect 7 letters only to give you four athletes.

FINISH

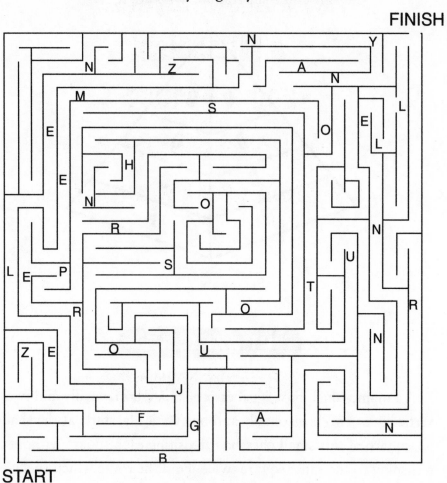

START

SEE ANSWER 160

At a doctor's surgery the waiting room was full. The doctor had arranged the appointment times in a special way and the appointments were 10 minutes apart. If Mr. Li has the next appointment in 10 minutes followed by Mr. Nike and then Mr. Lewis, in what order do Mr. Fischer, Mr. Becker and Mr. Schultz go into the surgery?

SEE ANSWER 166

Theo has four cars. He has a Toyota, a Mitsubishi and a Bentley. Is his fourth car a Nissan or a Peugeot?

SEE ANSWER 107

If the word PRESIDENTS is

Who are the other presidents?

SEE ANSWER 180

Move from square to touching square – including diagonals – to discover the name of a famous psychiatrist.

D	E	R	F
U	I	U	D
S	G	M	N

SEE ANSWER 11

PUZZLE 61

In a festival of music pieces, Schuller will be played at 2.00 pm, music by Verdi will be played at 5.06 pm and Schumann will be played at 11.00 pm. At what time will music by Offenbach be played?

SEE ANSWER 19

Rearrange each of the following groups to give the name of a politician or statesman. What are the four names?

IHANGD

ACTORS

HURLCLICH

ANAGRE

SEE ANSWER 60

The names of the following ten fashion designers can be found in this grid on vertical, horizontal and diagonal lines.
Can you find them?

Giorgio Armani

Calvin Klein

Hugo Boss

Bruce Oldfield

Jasper Conran

Red or Dead

Ellesse

Stussy

Gucci

Gianni Versace

Y	N	J	Z	B	W	K	X	B	T	N	F	G
G	I	O	R	G	I	O	A	R	M	A	N	I
T	E	S	S	O	B	O	G	U	H	R	G	A
X	L	V	E	S	V	R	Y	C	R	N	B	N
R	K	Q	S	H	F	X	B	E	V	O	K	N
Z	N	G	S	W	L	J	D	O	Q	C	M	I
J	I	T	E	M	P	O	F	L	W	R	Q	V
Y	V	K	L	K	R	S	B	D	Z	E	S	E
W	L	N	L	D	B	H	P	F	Q	P	D	R
F	A	T	E	G	U	C	C	I	X	S	Y	S
X	C	A	L	T	P	Q	M	E	H	A	W	A
V	D	G	J	V	Z	D	Y	L	G	J	Z	C
S	T	U	S	S	Y	F	K	D	B	J	B	E

SEE ANSWER 29

By taking a segment and finding its pair the names of four cities of the USA can be made. What are they?

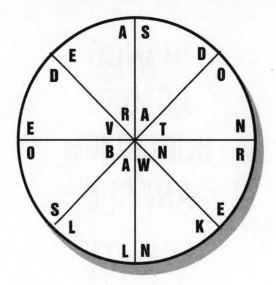

SEE ANSWER 39

PUZZLE 65

In a recipe book there are 8 recipes by Anton Mosimann, 9 by Raymond Blanc and 6 by Albert Roux.

How many Gary Rhodes recipes are there?

SEE ANSWER 45

The vowels have been missed out of the following groups of letters. Replace the vowels and rearrange each group to form the name of an American president. Who are the four presidents?

XNN
GRN
NNTLC
MNRT

SEE ANSWER 54

The names of three musical terms have been merged together here. What are they?

S	G	I	C	H	C
Z					E
R		P	C		E
E			L		A
Z	A	R	I		N
					T
O	O	O	T	D	T

SEE ANSWER 63

PUZZLE 68

If the country UNITED STATES is

♈ ♋ ☿ ♓ ♄ ♉   ♑ ♓ ♁ ⊙ ♓ ♄ ♑

Which are these states?

♋ ☿ ♋ ♋ ♄ ♑ ♍ ♓ ⊙

♓ ♄ ♅ ⊙ ♑

⊙ ♊ ⊙ ♑ ♃ ⊙

♄ ⊙ ♊ ☿ ♃ ♍ ♐ ♋ ☿ ⊙

♃ ♊ ♍ ♐ ☿ ♉ ⊙

♊ ♍ ♈ ☿ ♃ ♑ ☿ ⊙ ♋ ⊙

SEE ANSWER 68

PUZZLE 69

1B	1A	1D	5C		3D	1A	5C	4E	1D	3D
				▨						
2A	4A	2A	3B		3B	4D	2C	5A	2E	4A

The word frame above, when filled with the correct letters, will give the name of an athlete. The letters are arranged in the coded square below. There are two possible alternatives to fill each square of the word frame, one correct, the other incorrect. Who is the athlete?

	A	B	C	D	E
1	E	B	U	I	F
2	G	Q	V	J	R
3	H	D	T	S	C
4	A	T	K	U	E
5	L	N	L	P	U

SEE ANSWER 77

What letter is next in this sequence, and why?

C
D
L
N
?

SEE ANSWER 86

Four horses and their jockeys complete a race. Andrew wins the race. Marc is riding Blue Moon. While Redwing finishes last out of the four, Sunshine Boy wins the race. Marc finishes the race in second place. Dan finishes the race after John. Silver Shadow finishes the race after Blue Moon but before Redwing. Who is riding which horse and in what position do they finish?

SEE ANSWER 95

Louis drinks Bollinger champagne, wears Dior clothes, drives a Peugeot and wears a Seiko watch.

Does Louis like to watch Lewis or Tyson fight?

SEE ANSWER 100

Write the following five words related to music in the grid:

CHORD LENTO OPERA PITCH LARGO

When correctly arranged, another musical word will appear in the middle column. What is it?

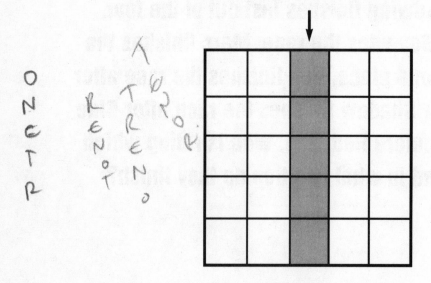

SEE ANSWER 112

PUZZLE 74

Can you work out what letter needs to be inserted in the middle to form four ancient gods, by combining opposite segments?

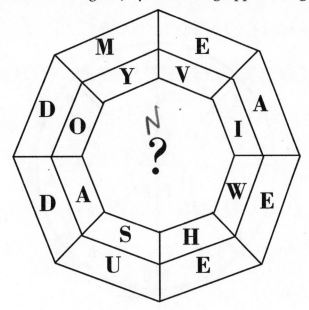

SEE ANSWER 121

PUZZLE 75

Complete the square with the letters of B R Y A N. When completed no row, column or diagonal line will contain the same letter more than once. One horizontal line will spell the name correctly. What letter should replace the question mark?

B	R	Y	A	N
Y	N	B	R	A
R	B	A	N	Y
A	N	R	Y	B
?	A	N	B	R

SEE ANSWER 128

PUZZLE 76

Take one letter from each segment to find the name of a film star.
Who is it?

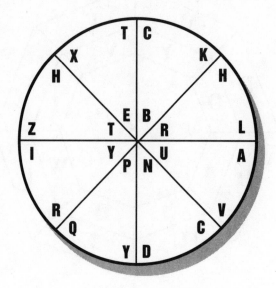

SEE ANSWER 136

PUZZLE 77

What two letters are missing (maybe more than once) from the
connected anagrams below and what is the connection?

REP - -

DGI - - -

RI - -

GRL - -

BURT - -

NTS - - -

SEE ANSWER 83

What letter is missing from the boxes below?

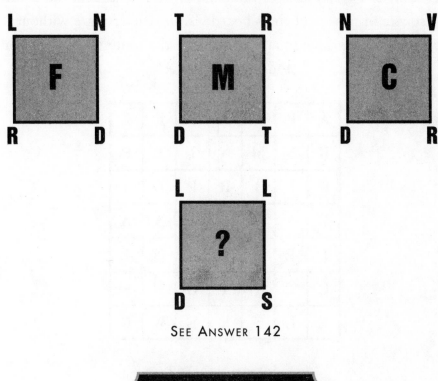

SEE ANSWER 142

Two sides of this pyramid, on a triangular base, can be seen the other one is obscured. Two six letter book names of the Bible are written around the figure. What are they?

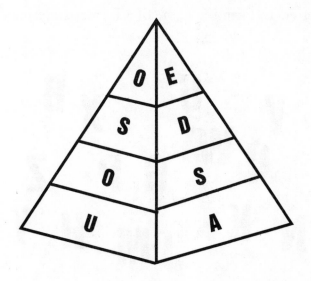

SEE ANSWER 147

A knight, which moves either one square horizontally and two vertically or two horizontally and one vertically, starts at the shaded square of this small chess board visiting each square without returning to the same square twice. Find the route which spells out four famous writers.

A	E	W	N	S	K	L
R	N	M	N	I	E	H
H	I	A	R	P	D	I
E	A	E	S	J	A	A
L	P	E	S	A	N	E
C	T	T	I	O	U	K
E	L	S	S	E	W	G

SEE ANSWER 152

Some letters are missing from this alphabet. Rearrange the missing letters to form the name of a former statesman.

V U X B
Q W G P Z
N K J M H Y

SEE ANSWER 6

A farmer gives names to his cows so that he knows which cows are for beef and which are for dairy products. If Daisy, Lady and Tess are all for dairy products and Mary, Olive and Carol are all for beef, what are Bunny, Ermitrude and Wilma to be used for?

SEE ANSWER 164

PUZZLE 83

This is an unusual maze. Find four separate routes through it without any route crossing another, although the paths may merge. On each route collect 6 letters to give you four musical terms.

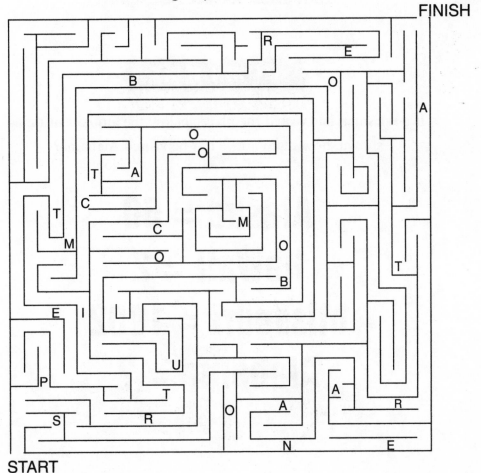

SEE ANSWER 158

Move from square to touching square – including diagonals – to discover the name of a singer-actress.

B	A	A	B
R	R	S	R
D	A	T	E
N	A	S	I

SEE ANSWER 14

If a salesman has visited the places below the amount of times shown, how many times has he visited Alabama?

Alaska = 50
Hawaii = 2
Missouri = 1002
Alabama = ?

SEE ANSWER 22

The names of the following ten furniture makers can be found in
this grid on either vertical, horizontal or diagonal lines.
Can you find them?

Adam

Chippendale

Cob

Gillow

Hepplewhite

Lock

Phillipponat

Seddon

Sheraton

Stuart

T	R	Y	J	P	Q	X	G	D	H	K	X
M	A	D	N	V	R	K	F	Z	F	W	Z
J	R	N	O	D	D	E	S	Y	J	O	T
P	S	N	O	T	A	R	E	H	S	Z	F
C	H	E	P	P	L	E	W	H	I	T	E
H	C	H	I	P	P	E	N	D	A	L	E
D	M	B	Y	Z	H	I	S	C	P	G	J
F	T	A	G	W	F	T	L	Y	I	B	M
X	U	K	D	D	U	O	D	L	N	T	X
M	V	C	P	A	C	K	L	W	I	G	K
K	W	G	R	K	M	O	V	R	U	H	Y
Z	H	T	R	X	W	W	B	N	Y	K	P

SEE ANSWER 32

PUZZLE 87

By taking a segment and finding its pair the names of three
scientists can be found. Who are they?

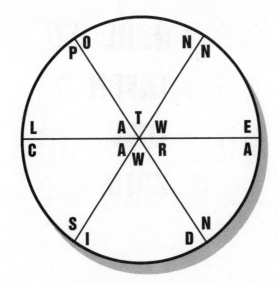

SEE ANSWER 42

There are 41 items of Chippendale furniture, 16 items by Adam and 30 items by Sheraton.

How many items by Gillow are there?

SEE ANSWER 48

The vowels have been missed out of the following groups of letters.
Replace the vowels and rearrange each group to form the
name of a composer. Who are the four composers?

NDHL

THVBN

LDVV

ZRTM

SEE ANSWER 57

PUZZLE 90

If the names DIEGO MARADONA and JACK CHARLTON are

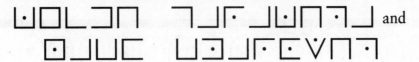 and

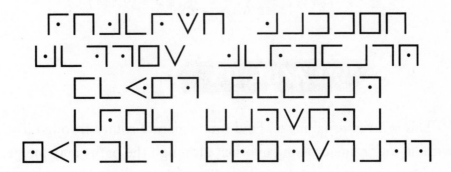

Who are the other footballers?

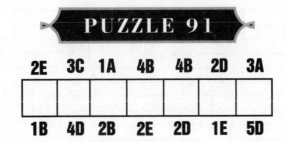

SEE ANSWER 71

PUZZLE 91

2E	3C	1A	4B	4B	2D	3A
1B	4D	2B	2E	2D	1E	5D

The wordframe above, when filled with the correct letters, will give the name of a city in the USA. The letters are arranged in the grid below. There are two possible alternatives to fill each square of the wordframe, one correct, the other incorrect. What is the city?

	A	B	C	D	E
1	I	D	B	F	T
2	Y	N	Q	G	C
3	V	J	H	R	X
4	M	A	E	K	P
5	C	Z	S	O	U

SEE ANSWER 80

What letter should appear next in this series?

(2) (C) (5) (F) (10) (K) (14) (0) (18) (S) (20) (U) (25) (?)

SEE ANSWER 89

PUZZLE 93

This is an unusual maze. Find four separate routes through it without any route crossing another, although the paths may merge. On each route collect six letters to give you four scientists. Who are they?

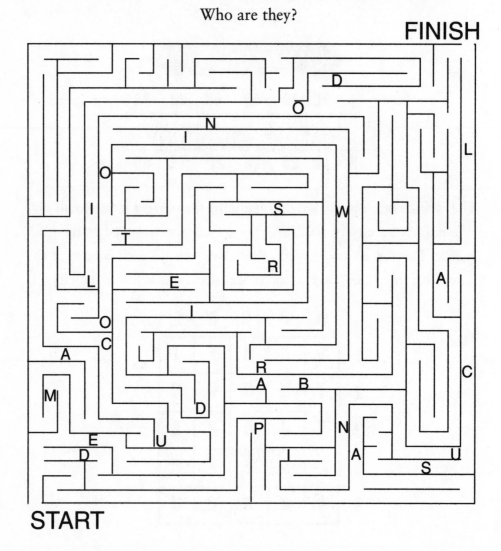

SEE ANSWER 161

Turn the dials on this diagram to give 8 forenames and 8 surnames of famous actresses. Then match them up to give their full names. Who are they? (A score above 5 is very good!)

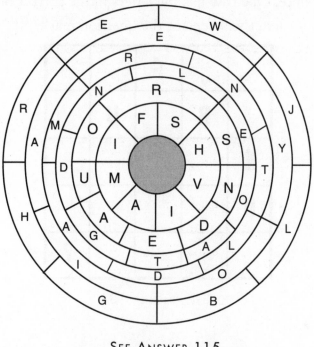

SEE ANSWER 115

PUZZLE 95

Can you work out what letter needs to be inserted in the middle to form four airlines by combining opposite segments?

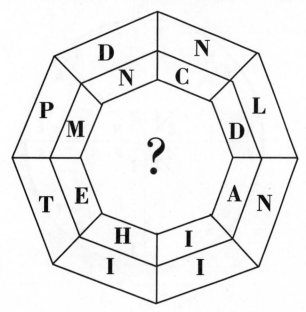

SEE ANSWER 124

PUZZLE 96

Complete the square using the letters of FREUD. When completed no row, column or diagonal line should contain the same letter more than once. One row has the letters in the correct order. What letter will replace the question mark?

		F		
	R		U	
E				
D				
				?

SEE ANSWER 131

PUZZLE 97

Collect one letter from each segment to give the name of a pop star. Who is it?

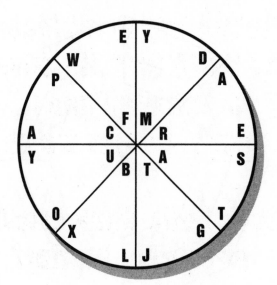

SEE ANSWER 139

54

A knight, which moves either one square horizontally and two vertically or two horizontally and one vertically, is positioned on this chess board on position A1. If you move to all the squares in the right sequence, without visiting any square twice, you will find the names of five famous golfers.

O	P	C	A	O	R	N
K	A	T	Y	I	P	D
L	M	L	R	C	N	A
R	P	I	Y	M	L	D
W	A	E	K	N	G	O
R	N	E	T	C	L	A
R	A	I	O	F	S	E

SEE ANSWER 155

Rolfe likes Demi Moore and Steffi Graf. He drives a Vauxhall and wears a Casio watch.

Does Rolfe drink Lanson or Laurent Perrier?

SEE ANSWER 103

A round of drinks were on a table. Alvin had a Martini, Eric had a Pernod and Roger had a Brandy. Can you match the other drinks to people? Tia Maria, Vodka, Rum, Whiskey, Ursula, Olga, Harry, Ian.

SEE ANSWER 167

PUZZLE 101

The names of the following ten film stars can be found in this grid on vertical, horizontal and diagonal lines. Can you find them?

John Cleese

Tom Cruise

Mel Gibson

Hugh Grant

Tom Hanks

Val Kilmer

Bruce Lee

Al Pacino

Sean Penn

Brad Pitt

W	Z	Q	E	P	R	V	H	E	F	M
T	O	U	S	Y	J	A	H	E	E	Z
T	N	S	I	G	K	L	U	L	S	W
I	I	E	U	F	H	K	G	E	E	P
P	C	A	R	H	X	I	H	C	E	H
D	A	N	C	H	B	L	G	U	L	J
A	P	P	M	S	Q	M	R	R	C	R
R	L	E	O	J	R	E	A	B	N	G
B	A	N	T	T	Z	R	N	P	H	Y
S	K	N	A	H	M	O	T	W	O	S
Y	R	B	X	F	Q	J	X	N	J	S

SEE ANSWER 35

In a gallery, painting number 2105 is by Edvard Munch, painting number 1650 is by Claude Monet and painting number 151 is by Pablo Picasso.

What number is the painting by Salvador Dali?

SEE ANSWER 25

How far should it be to Las Vegas on this strange signpost?

290 HOUSTON

CINCINNATI 420

420 LOS ANGELES

LAS VEGAS ?

SEE ANSWER 51

PUZZLE 104

If the name ELIZABETH TAYLOR is

Who are the other legendary film stars?

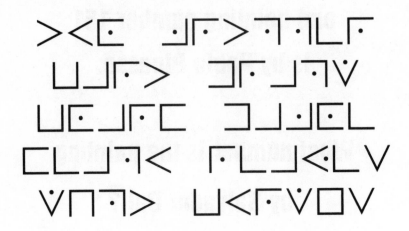

SEE ANSWER 74

PUZZLE 105

Two series are merged together here. Which two letters should appear next in this series?

D V H Q L L P G T ? ?

SEE ANSWER 92

Lena drives a Volkswagen. She wears White Linen perfume and her preferred chef is Gary Rhodes. Who would be her first choice dress designer, Jasper Conran or Jurgen Lehl?

SEE ANSWER 106

PUZZLE 107

Turn the dials on this diagram to reveal 13 musical terms. A score above 8 is very good.

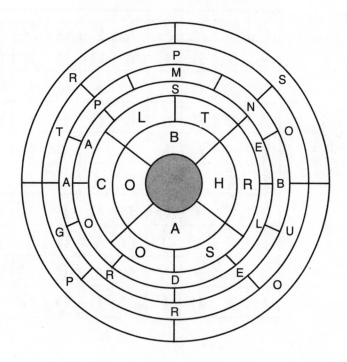

SEE ANSWER 118

George Michael has sold 1151 CDs, Bruce Springsteen has sold 101 and Simple Minds have sold 2552. How many have Simply Red sold?

SEE ANSWER 26

PUZZLE 109

The names of the following ten car manufacturers can be found in this grid on vertical, horizontal and diagonal lines. Can you find them?

Citroen

Jaguar

Peugeot

Renault

Rolls Royce

Rover

Skoda

Toyota

Volkswagen

Yugo

R	N	B	L	F	K	X	C	D	R
E	N	D	C	W	Q	H	S	O	E
N	E	G	A	W	S	K	L	O	V
A	O	H	J	K	O	L	B	P	O
U	R	G	V	D	S	F	Y	J	R
L	T	C	A	R	A	U	G	A	J
T	I	T	O	E	G	U	E	P	M
P	C	Y	T	O	Y	O	T	A	B
J	C	F	V	G	Z	C	W	D	K
E	K	D	P	M	H	Q	G	Y	F

SEE ANSWER 36

Some letters are missing from this alphabet. Rearrange the missing letters to form the name of a river.

C F I W O U X
J V Q R K
L P B M S H
D

SEE ANSWER 4

Complete the square using the letters of T E X A S. When completed no row, column or diagonal line should contain the same letter more than once. One horizontal line will spell the name correctly. What letter will replace the question mark?

			T	
		E	X	
		A		
	S			
		X		?

SEE ANSWER 129

PUZZLE 112

Collect one letter from each segment to give the
name of a book in the Bible. What is it?

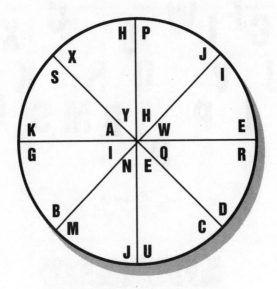

SEE ANSWER 137

PUZZLE 113

What letter has been missed from the last box?

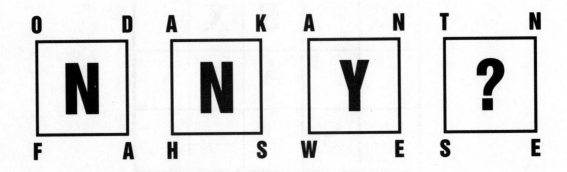

SEE ANSWER 143

Move from square to touching square – including diagonals – to discover the name of an American state.

E	P	N	S
I	N	Y	L
A	N	A	V

SEE ANSWER 12

PUZZLE 115

A bar sold

500 measures of brandy,

1000 measures of rum

and just 1 measure of Gin.

How many measures of

whiskey did it sell?

SEE ANSWER 20

The names of the following ten watch manufacturers can be found in this grid on vertical, horizontal and diagonal lines. Can you find them?

Casio

Gucci

Ingersoll

Limit

Rotary

Rolex

Seiko

Sekonda

Timex

Tissot

H	P	C	T	U	B	O	P	M	I
G	U	C	C	I	Q	K	F	N	J
M	B	K	W	T	M	I	G	T	C
J	N	P	A	C	O	E	Z	D	V
Q	X	V	D	A	R	S	X	Q	Y
Z	R	X	N	S	F	X	S	K	R
D	K	E	O	I	M	B	F	I	A
V	X	L	K	O	L	I	M	I	T
P	L	O	E	Y	Q	W	J	V	O
J	F	R	S	B	M	K	U	P	R

SEE ANSWER 30

By taking a segment and finding its pair, four film stars can be found. Who are they?

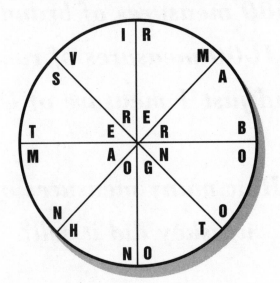

SEE ANSWER 40

IDENTITY CRISIS

It is now the year AD 2482, and Universe War II has just finished. You were only a baby when the war began and you were left on Earth because it was the safest planet. During the war it was realized that your parents were leaders of the Secret Service and they were pursued from planet to planet, so they completely lost touch with you. You therefore know nothing of your origins and are only known by the symbol §. You have a natural desire to go in search of your parents and find your identity. You hire a Planet Hopper and, not wishing to travel alone, find three friends who are willing to help in the search for your given name.

You must travel to many planets in the Universe, some more than once, picking up clues each time you stop. Answer the first question to discover the direction to travel and which planet you should go to first. Each question should be answered in order. All the answers are on page 80. To move from one planet to another you must follow the direction of the arrows on the map. Your Planet Hopper can travel across a maximum of three planets on its route, but it must stop on the fourth one to check fuel levels. You may not pass the fourth planet. At each stop collect the number shown on the planet.

Good luck.

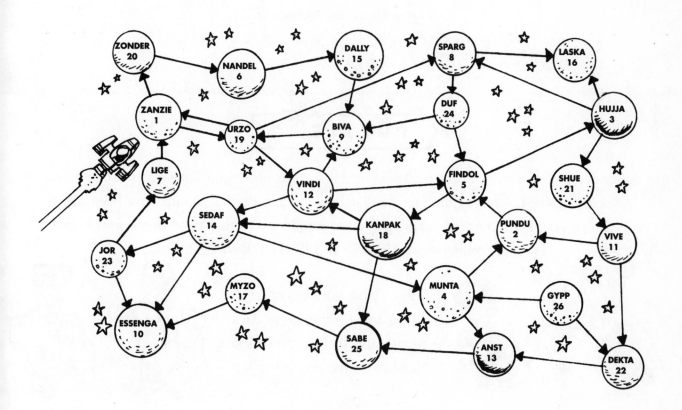

The initials of compass directions form a series.
What direction should replace the question mark?

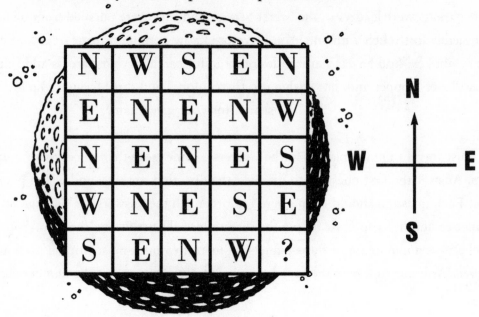

N	W	S	E	N
E	N	E	N	W
N	E	N	E	S
W	N	E	S	E
S	E	N	W	?

If you think the answer is:

a) S, go to Shue   b) W, go to Sedaf   c) N, go to Hujja

SEE ANSWER 4

Since the end of the 24th century, some names have been written differently. Your friend named MBNNH, who is riding in the Planet Hopper with you, would have been called Naomi a couple of hundred years ago. What would your other two friends and Planet Hopper companions, AFMJSP and IPRITB, have been called?

If you think the answer is:
a) Julius and Daniel, go to Anst
b) Benito and Joshua, go to Sparg
c) Benita and Joanne, go to Jor

SEE ANSWER 8

Shortly after landing, you meet someone who claims to know your parents but, after much wasted time, you discover the person is a trickster and you have to move on in your search. To discover what you will eat for your first meal after leaving Earth, rearrange the order of the following car manufacturers and place them in the grid below, and the name of a food can be read along the shaded diagonal.

HONDA   CITROEN   ISUZU   PORSCHE   MAZDA

What is it ?

If you think the answer is:

a) Pasta, go to Lask   b) Curry, go to Gypp   c) Pizza, go to Kanpak

SEE ANSWER 12

{ PUZZLE 4 }

Your Planet Hopper is equipped with a selection of champagne for celebrating new information. Add the same two letters to each of the following groups and rearrange each one to form the name of a champagne.
Which two letters must be added?

TUNAR   NITTGATE   THONE   CREEM

If you think the answer is:

a) I and R, go to Biva   b) R and E, go to Munta   c) E and I, go to Sabe

SEE ANSWER 15

PUZZLE 5

How far should it be to Shue
according to this strange signpost?

If you think the answer is:
   a) 700, go to Urzo
   b) 600, go to Sparg
   c) 625, go to Essenga

SEE ANSWER 21

PUZZLE 6

You manage to find records of a person known by the same symbol as yourself.
Your hopes are high that this person may be a relative. Investigations enable you to
trace § but, on visiting him, you cannot find any connection or reason to believe
you are connected. You must, therefore, move on.

Pyramids have been discovered on other planets besides Earth. The pyramid visible
from your Planet Hopper was dedicated to two eight-letter famous composers.
Their names are written around the pyramid but two sides are obscured.

If you think the missing letters to complete the names are:
   a) L, K, T, A, P, Z, F and E, go to Anst
   b) P, A, N, I, S, U, B and T, go to Zonder
   c) T, N, I, R, S, M, O and H, if so go to Vive

SEE ANSWER 27

While you travel, you and your friends enjoy watching old movies. Place one letter in the middle of this diagram so that the surname of an actor or actress can be rearranged from each straight line of letters. The added letter will be the last letter of each film star's name.

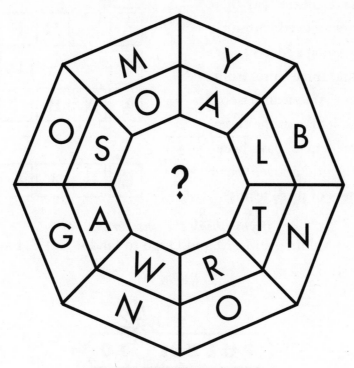

If you think the answer is:

a) I, go to Myzo   b) T, go to Dekta   c) E, go to Biva

SEE ANSWER 17

PUZZLE 8

If the countries ARTRONE, LOL and BIJOU are to be found on JOR, on which planet will you find the countries BEOTT, PZE, AXRID and AEDUOUS?

If you think the answer is:
a) Findol, go to Gypp
b) Urzo, go to Zanzie
c) Sabe, go to Nandel

SEE ANSWER 11

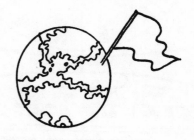

At Information Central you find records going back five years, which show an address on the other side of the planet for your parents. You travel all the way there only to find that they moved without leaving a forwarding address.

You do, however, find three shirts from different Major League American Baseball teams on Earth. The letters of the three clubs, each with nine letters, have been merged together in the grid above. Which are the middle letters of these teams?

M	L	E	I	E	S
N					T
A		M	E		V
O			D		O
N	N	R	I		L
					E
C	B	A	L	A	T

If you think the answer is:

a) L, T and N, go to Munta   b) L, M and O, go to Findol   c) E, I and E, go to Sedaf

SEE ANSWER 24

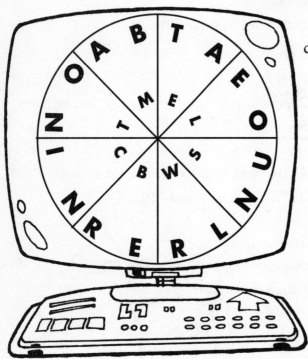

You are now in a jam, so you consult your computer. The screen gives the information shown left, and tells you to look at the library in the shuttle for clues. Four of the authors' surnames can be found by pairing segments.

If you think their first names are:
a) Ed, George, Emily and Jane,
    go to Zanzie
b) Sigmund, Bernard, William and Agatha,
    go to Shue
c) Sheila, Oscar, John and Arthur,
    go to Sabe

SEE ANSWER 3

In return for an address where your parents were staying about a year ago, you are asked to solve a problem. You must complete the grid with the letters A, B, C, D and E, so that no vertical, horizontal or diagonal line contains the same letter more than once. What letter should replace the question mark?

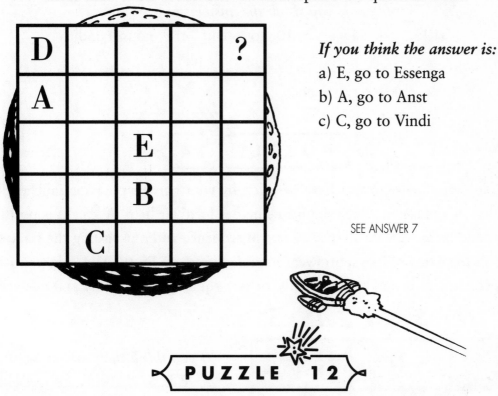

If you think the answer is:
a) E, go to Essenga
b) A, go to Anst
c) C, go to Vindi

SEE ANSWER 7

A female, who seems to be very kind and helpful, says she is a good friend of your mother. She boards your Planet Hopper, then takes you round and round in circles before you realize she is completely insane and you are no nearer to finding your parents. Once again, you are hopelessly lost and decide that you must either spin a coin or find another way to find your next planet. You and your three friends have a game of anagrams. In this game, you can only form nicknames of NFL Football teams. The four groups of letters are:

SLEAGE   GLENABS   PLODHINS   SJTE

You trust that your luck is with you. If you think their names begin with:
a) A, N, S and T, go to Zonder   b) E, B, D and J go to Findol
c) L, E, H and S, go to Kanpak

SEE ANSWER 20

PUZZLE 13

You spend several days on Findol finding information about your parents' movements. You spend 10 days in the country Vuovu, 1 day in Eit and 5 days in Zafov. How many days do you spend in Kanax?

If you think the answer is:
a) 15, go to Hujja   b) 10, go to Duf   c) 9, go to Pundu

SEE ANSWER 18

PUZZLE 14

You are told that a message may have been left by your parents on a special chess board. It has been left in a museum which thanks its heroes for their help. A knight is positioned on square A1 and by moving to all the squares in sequence without visiting the same square twice, it spells the name of five sportswear manufacturers on Earth. The knight moves either one square horizontally and two vertically, or two squares horizontally and one vertically.

	1	2	3	4	5
A	P	S	A	R	M
B	O	O	U	U	D
C	A	E	K	A	E
D	R	B	I	I	M
E	K	D	B	E	N

If you think their names begin with:
a) P, E, S, U and N, go to Dekta
b) P, D, E, N and I go to Laska
c) P, N, A, U and R, go to Zanzie

SEE ANSWER 28

PUZZLE 15

You are feeling disheartened, but your friends keep your spirits high and make you determined not to give up. You are given another address where your parents were known to have been until a year ago. At this address they have left an address of an aunt. Unfortunately, your aunt is not living on the same planet, so you set off again. You decide to stop on other planets to collect information on your way.

There is a problem with the Planet Hopper. The oxygen filters are not working properly and only one metal can be used to mend them. The name of the metal is missed out of the alphabet written below. What is the metal?

B C D E F G H J K O Q R S V W X Y Z

If you think the metal begins with:
a) P, go to Sedaf   b) A, go to Vive   c) M, go to Lige

SEE ANSWER 22

PUZZLE 16

You are sent to a bar where friends of your parents are said to drink.

You do not have any luck in finding them but the four of you stop for a drink anyway. IPRITB is drinking Campari and MBNNH is drinking Rum.

If you think AFMJSP is drinking:
a) Whiskey, go to Sabe
b) Daiquiri, go to Nandel
c) Tequila, go to Munta

SEE ANSWER 10

PUZZLE 17

A couple of your friends are suffering a little radiation sickness (they swear it has nothing to do with last night's drinking!). You ask one of the strange-looking locals for advice on medication.

He tells you to add one letter to each of the following groups so that each group can be rearranged to give a name. The seven names are connected. He tells you to then place together the seven added letters and they will give the name of the medication you need.

CLBK   HONNOJ   CERE   STRICHE
CRENTOE   TAAOU   GLENLU

If you think the medication is:

a) Linctus, go to Myzo   b) Steroid, go to Dally   c) Aspirin, go to Findol

SEE ANSWER 25

PUZZLE 18

When you see your aunt she is unable to give you your parents' address, but she does give you the address of a relative you didn't know you had who will know it.

You now have information about the breed of your parents' dog. The breed is written in the coded square to the right. If the word frame is completed with the correct letters it will give the name of the breed. There are two possible alternatives to fill each square of the wordframe, one correct the other incorrect.

What is the breed of your parents' dog?

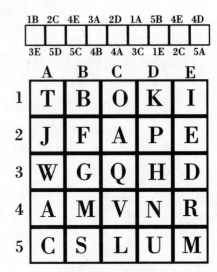

If the dog is:

a) Spotted, go to Kanpak

b) Long-haired, go to Shue

c) Black all over, go to Gypp

SEE ANSWER 14

PUZZLE 19

Your electronic watch will tell you the time and temperature on other planets.
On Nandel, it is 2 o'clock and 36°, on Myzo, it is 1 o'clock and 27°, and on Essenga,
it is 3 o'clock and 36°. What time and temperature will it be on Jor?

If you think the answer is:

a) 5 o'clock and 42°, go to Pundu   b) 1 o'clock and 18°, then go to Jor
c) 2 o'clock and 29°, go to Hujja

SEE ANSWER 2

PUZZLE 20

Most of the people you meet are very friendly and do their best to
remember anything which may be helpful to you. But it is such a shame
that there is interplanetary hatred. For instance, the Melony
people from Myzo detest the Noya people from Nandel, and the
Sinach people from Shue cannot tolerate the Dazza people.

Where are the Dazza people from?
a) Dekta, if so go to Munta
b) Dally, if so go to Zanzie
c) Sedaf, if so go to Vive

SEE ANSWER 6

PUZZLE 21

As you arrive for another visit to this planet, the locals are trying to stage a musical you have seen in London, Earth. You are able to help them in exchange for more help with your mission. Move from square to touching square to find the name of the musical.

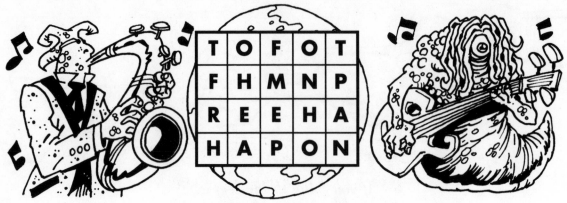

What is the first letter of the name?

a) P, if so go to Urzo   b) H, if so go to Laska   c) T, if so go to Sedaf

SEE ANSWER 23

PUZZLE 22

Many of the people you and your friends meet have heard stories of Ancient Greece. You assume that it must have been from your parents, and they wish to know more about it. In their language SOCRATES is written

Would the fourth letters of the following names be:

a) A, I, P, and N, if so go to Dekta   b) A, T, C and S, if so go to Shue

c) R, A, J and O, if so go to Sparg

SEE ANSWER 26

You are told that your parents have left behind an expensive painting, which they brought from Earth. Rearrange the following list of scientists so that the name of the artist can be read down the third column.

FARADAY
BROWN
GALILEO
NEWTON
THALES
FAHRENHEIT

If you think his name begins with:

a) W, go to Biva   b) R, go to Anst   c) H, go to Sabe

SEE ANSWER 19

You go to the address given to you by your aunt, only to find it is a boarding school. There is a child there who looks very similar to you, and after carrying out a gene test you discover he is a brother you didn't know you had. He is suspicious of you and while he gives you a helping hand in finding your parents, he will not give you an address or exact directions.

Before you leave this planet you meet some of the superbeings who live there. They are happy to see you because they are stuck on a super-intellectual puzzle. They know the letters on the triangles are connected with a place on Earth but they need your help. What letter will replace the question mark on the third triangle?

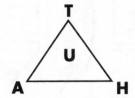 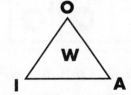 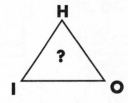

If you think the answer is:

a) T, go to Myzo   b) O, go to Sedaf   c) G, go to Essenga

SEE ANSWER 16

Word of your search now precedes you, and you are being tested before you can proceed. You are asked to replace the vowels in the following groups of letters to read three connected 10-letter words. The three items will be found in the same area of your Planet Hopper.

CNNLLN   MYNNS   GRGNZL

Do you think they will be found in:

a) the kitchen area, if so go to Lige

b) the washroom area, if so go to Sparg

c) the sleeping area, if so go to Kanpak

SEE ANSWER 9

You see the following direction indicator which, when followed correctly, leads you to a place name familiar from Earth. Start in the top left corner.

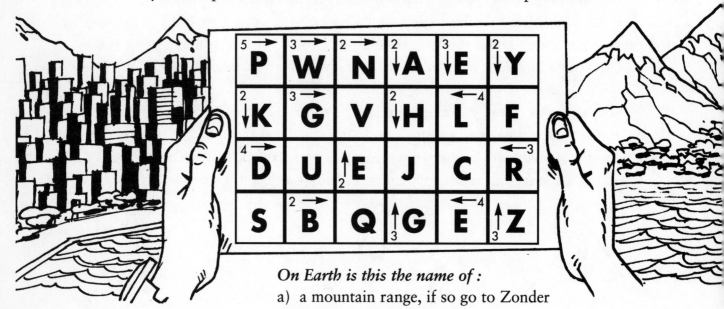

On Earth is this the name of :

a) a mountain range, if so go to Zonder

b) a city, if so go to Duf

c) an ocean, if so go to Biva

SEE ANSWER 13

While looking through record books you have seen the populations of six of the planets. Sparg has the second highest population and Biva has the second lowest. Munta has a lower population than Vindi but higher than Dekta. Pundu has a higher population than Biva but lower than Munta.

Placing the planets in order of highest to lowest population, what order will they be in?

a) Munta, Sparg, Vindi, Pundu, Biva, Dekta, if so go to Hujja
b) Vindi, Sparg, Munta, Pundu, Biva, Dekta, if so go to Dally
c) Pundu, Sparg, Munta, Dekta, Biva, Vindi, if so go to Jor

SEE ANSWER 1

PUZZLE 28

If you have successfully followed the clues, you will receive the following message when you land on this planet.

If you think the 20th letter of the message is
a) V, go to Gypp   b) Z, go to Munta   c) N, go to Sedaf

SEE ANSWER 5

DESTINATION

If you have arrived on Sedaf, CONGRATULATIONS.
You and your parents are reunited. Your name will become obvious when
you replace each number collected from your 28 stops on the planets with
the letter that appears in that alphabetical place.
What is your name?

ANSWERS

1 *b)*

2 *b) The number of vowels in the planet name gives the time. The number of consonants multiplied by 9 gives the temperature.*

3 *a) The surnames are Austen, Orwell, Bronte and McBain.*

4 *c) The series N, E, N, W, S, E is written down the first column and up the second, etc.*

5 *c) The message says, "Your parents are waiting for you."*

6 *b) The first and last letters of the race of people are the same as the first and second letters of the planet.*

7 *c)*

D	E	A	B	C
A	B	C	D	E
C	D	E	A	B
E	A	B	C	D
B	C	D	E	A

8 *b) Replace the first, third and fifth letter of each name with the one that follows it in the alphabet, and replace the second, fourth and sixth letter with the one that precedes it in the alphabet.*

9 *a) The words are Cannelloni, Mayonnaise and Gorgonzola.*

10 *c) The last letter of the drink is the same as the first letter of the name.*

11 *b) The middle letters of the countries in reverse order spell out the name of the planet.*

12 *c) The order of the words is: Porsche, Citroen, Mazda, Isuzu and Honda.*

13 *a) The mountain range is Pyrenees.*

14 *a) The dog is a Dalmatian.*

15 *a) The champagnes are Ruinart, Taittinger, Henriot and Mercier.*

16 *b) American States are written on the triangles; Utah, Iowa and Ohio.*

17 *c) The film stars are Wayne, Gable, Stone and Moore.*

18 *b) The Roman numerals in each name are added together to give the number of days.*

19 *a) The artist is Warhol.*

20 *b) The nicknames are Eagles, Bengals, Dolphins and Jets.*

21 *a) In each planet name a consonant is given a value of 225 and a vowel is given a value of 125. These are added together to give the distance.*

22 *a) The metal is platinum.*

23 *a) The musical is "Phantom of the Opera".*

24 *c) The teams are Cleveland, Baltimore, Minnesota.*

25 *c) The drug needed is Aspirin and the linked people are athletes, Black, Johnson, Perec, Christie, Torrence, Aouita and Gunnell.*

26 *c) The names are Sparta, Titan, Trojan and Acropolis.*

27 *b) The composers are Paganini and Schubert.*

28 *c) The sportswear manufacturers are Puma, Nike, Adidas, Umbro and Reebok.*

Your name appears on page 128, at the end of the Answers section.

Along a street there are 7 Ford cars, 9 Toyota cars and 13 Alfa Romeo cars.

How many Mazda cars are there?

SEE ANSWER 46

PUZZLE 119

The vowels have been missed out of the following groups of letters. Replace the vowels and rearrange each group to form the name of a film star. Who are the four stars?

STND FFMHN

VST RNMT

TRCPK YZSW

LMN FFGTHRS

SEE ANSWER 55

The names of three lakes have been merged together here.
Which are they?

SEE ANSWER 64

PUZZLE 121

If the term ANCIENT GODS is

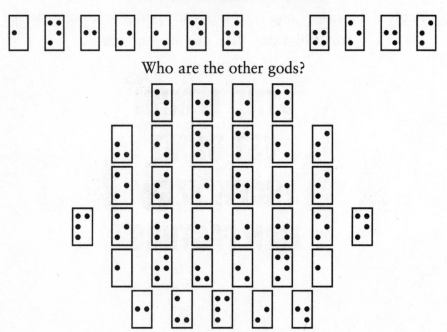

Who are the other gods?

SEE ANSWER 69

1E	2C	3D		3A	4E	2D	5D	3B	1C
4A	5B	1B		1C	5B	4E	2C	4C	3D

The word frame above, when filled with the correct letters, will give the name of a film star. The letters are arranged in the coded square below. There are two possible alternatives to fill each square of the word frame, one correct, the other incorrect. Who is the film star?

	A	B	C	D	E
1	A	L	R	F	M
2	Q	J	E	H	C
3	G	Y	P	N	W
4	D	Z	O	K	B
5	T	I	V	S	X

SEE ANSWER 78

What letters are missing from this sequence?

A S ? ? G H J

SEE ANSWER 87

Six people go into a store through the underground car park going to floors 1, 2, 3, 4, 5 and 6. Each person goes to a different floor in the same elevator, which goes up stopping at each floor. Eddie's ride is the longest. Angie gets out before Frankie but after Debbie. Charlie gets out first. Barbie leaves before Debbie, who leaves at the third floor.

At what floor does each person leave?

SEE ANSWER 96

Jean is a relation of the scientist Jenner. Jean was born in Denver but now lives in Seattle.

Is Jean is a bigger fan of tennis player Sampras or McEnroe?

SEE ANSWER 101

PUZZLE 126

The people listed below were told that they could win a car if they could arrange their names in the grid below to give the car's manufacturer down the shaded column. What car did they get? Their names were:

BRUCE DIANA SARAH BRIAN BILLY MARIE

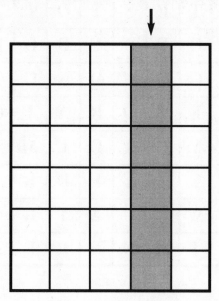

See Answer 113

PUZZLE 127

Two sides of this pyramid can be seen, but the other two are obscured. Two eight-letter American states are written around the pyramid. What are they?

See Answer 148

A knight, which moves either one square horizontally and two vertically or two horizontally and one vertically, starts at the shaded square of this chess board visiting each square without returning to the same square twice. Find the route which spells out six famous movie stars.

O	T	E	S	I	O	T	I
M	O	P	S	L	B	G	R
E	O	G	N	D	N	G	O
N	E	B	O	R	A	I	O
H	V	E	J	D	L	M	T
S	R	A	E	F	D	R	N
E	W	B	U	A	I	R	C
O	I	M	N	E	R	E	T

SEE ANSWER 153

This list of English monarchs shows the fictitious number of years they reigned. Can you think of a monarch who would have reigned for less than a year?

Mary	**17**
James	**12**
George	**10**
Charles	**7**
William	**3**

SEE ANSWER 170

In a large raffle
Ian had ticket number one, Vivian had number twelve and David had number 1006.

Who of the following had ticket numbers 500, 60, 1000 and 151 from Axel, Charlie, Brenda and Norman?

SEE ANSWER 165

Some letters are missing from this alphabet. Rearrange the missing letters to form the name of a European city.

M W D
Y Z Q P
I
L O K J V
X F G N

SEE ANSWER 7

Move from square to touching square – including diagonals – to discover the name of a car.

O	R	L	K
B	A	G	N
M	H	I	I

SEE ANSWER 15

PUZZLE 133

If Beckenbauer made 100 appearances for his country and Littbarski made 52 and Völler made 105, how many appearances did Hässler make?

SEE ANSWER 23

The names of the following ten perfumes can be found in this grid on vertical, horizontal and diagonal lines. Can you find them?

Amarige
Anais Anais
Coco
Dune
Miss Dior
Obsession
Paris
Safari
Samsara
Spellbound

S	I	A	N	A	S	I	A	N	A
A	P	D	G	H	F	P	J	C	R
F	C	E	G	I	R	A	M	A	A
A	F	H	L	D	J	R	K	F	S
R	Y	Q	U	L	Z	I	Z	R	M
I	R	N	Z	X	B	S	F	X	A
Q	E	V	K	W	O	O	Y	J	S
B	H	K	V	D	W	C	U	G	I
O	B	S	E	S	S	I	O	N	G
R	O	I	D	S	S	I	M	C	D

SEE ANSWER 33

*If there have been
13 Malaysia Airline flights,
22 Virgin Atlantic flights and
16 Pan Am flights this week,
how many Cathay Pacific
flights have there been?*

SEE ANSWER 49

The names of five pop groups are written here in code.
What are they?

i) **10 6 22 22 13**

ii) **8 18 14 11 15 2 9 22 23**

iii) **25 12 13 17 12 5 18**

iv) **20 22 13 22 8 18 8**

v) **8 18 14 11 15 22 14 18 13 23 8**

SEE ANSWER 72

PUZZLE 137

What letter should appear next in this series?

A E F H I K ?

SEE ANSWER 90

Olga lives in Canada and attended the University of Winnipeg. She most enjoys listening to singer George Michael.

Is her perfume Coco or Dune?

SEE ANSWER 104

PUZZLE 139

Turn the dial on this diagram to give 11 names of lakes from around the world. (7 or over is a good score.)

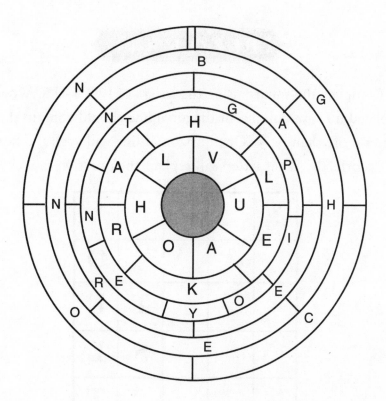

SEE ANSWER 116

PUZZLE 140

Can you work out what letter needs to be inserted in the middle to form four artists by combining opposite segments?

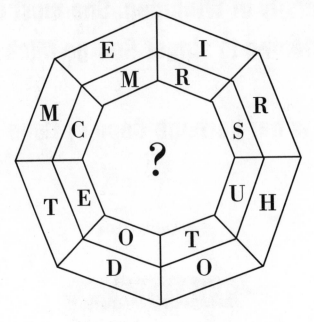

SEE ANSWER 125

PUZZLE 141

Complete the square using the letters of L O T U S. When completed no row, column or diagonal line should contain the same letter more than once. One horizontal line will spell the flower correctly. What letter will replace the question mark?

?				
				O
			T	U
			S	L
				T

SEE ANSWER 132

PUZZLE 142

Some letters are missing from this alphabet. Rearrange the missing letters to form the name of a Mexican city.

SEE ANSWER 5

PUZZLE 143

If the owner of the Mercedes is Dave, the owner of the Nissan is Simon and the owner of the Porsche is Colin, can you find the owners of the remaining cars from the people listed?

Cars: Toyota, Rover, Jaguar, Fiat and Honda.

People: Nigel, Irene, Vera, Oliver and Ursula.

SEE ANSWER 168

If Mercury is linked with Fillmore, Jupiter with Carter, Saturn with Ford and Uranus with Arthur, which of the following presidents would be linked with Charon?

i) **Lincoln**

ii) **Adams**

iii) **Monroe**

iv) **Buchanan**

v) **Hoover**

SEE ANSWER 173

If London has 550 visitors, Budapest has 500 and Madrid has 2001, how many visitors does Paris have?

SEE ANSWER 21

The names of the following ten tennis players can be found in this grid on vertical, horizontal and diagonal lines. Can you find them?

Jeremy Bates

Pat Cash

Wayne Ferreira

Ivan Lendl

Jana Novotna

Marc Rosset

Greg Rusedski

Monica Seles

Michael Stich

Helena Sukova

C	J	H	J	K	I	M	F	G	I	M	C	W
B	E	C	M	Z	K	Y	X	B	V	N	A	Y
J	R	I	A	O	S	J	V	H	A	Y	V	S
F	E	T	R	N	D	C	Y	V	N	D	O	E
K	M	S	C	H	E	P	H	E	L	K	K	L
G	Y	L	R	D	S	K	F	P	E	J	U	E
Z	B	E	O	X	U	E	G	A	N	M	S	S
C	A	A	S	W	R	W	B	T	D	D	A	A
P	T	H	S	R	G	M	W	C	L	Z	N	C
J	E	C	E	F	E	Y	V	A	Y	B	E	I
F	S	I	T	Y	R	Z	M	S	J	X	L	N
H	R	M	P	H	G	C	B	H	K	F	E	O
A	N	T	O	V	O	N	A	N	A	J	H	M

SEE ANSWER 31

By taking a segment and finding its pair the names of four musical terms can be found. What are they?

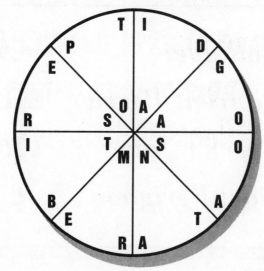

SEE ANSWER 41

The vowels have been missed out of the following groups of letters. Replace the vowels and rearrange each group to form the name of a female singer. Who are the four singers?

NN LNXN

NJT CSKJN

RHM RYC

KLY GMN

Sᴇᴇ Aɴsᴡᴇʀ 56

The price of champagne in a store in England is shown here.
How much will Dom Perignon cost?

Bollinger	*£9.40*
Laurent Perrier	*£18.00*
Perrier Jouet	*£16.00*
Dom Perignon	*£ ?*

Sᴇᴇ Aɴsᴡᴇʀ 47

The names of two actors have been merged together here.
Who are they?

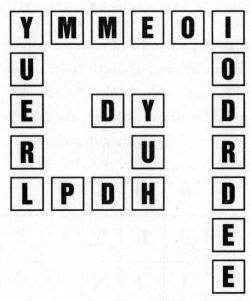

SEE ANSWER 65

If the word SCIENTIST is

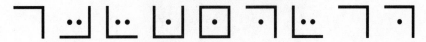

who are these scientists?

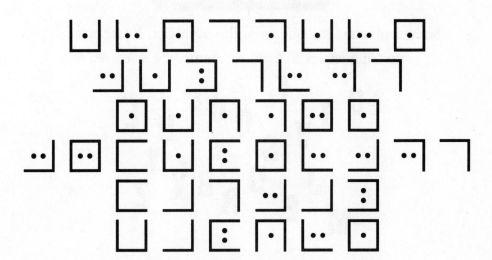

SEE ANSWER 70

1D	2A	5E		2C	3B	2E	4B	5A	1A	1B	4A
2C	4B	3B		1E	4C	1A	3D	2C	3E	4D	5C

The word frame above, when filled with the correct letters, will give the name of a female athlete. The letters are arranged in the coded square below. There are two possible alternatives to fill each square of the word frame, one correct, the other incorrect.

Who is the athlete?

	A	B	C	D	E
1	G	A	B	L	S
2	I	Q	M	F	C
3	D	Z	X	O	K
4	H	J	C	W	M
5	L	V	N	P	R

SEE ANSWER 79

Some letters are missing from this alphabet. Rearrange the missing letters to form the name of a scientist.

SEE ANSWER 1

What letter should appear next in this series?

M V E M J S U N

SEE ANSWER 88

Complete the square using the letters of L E W I S. When completed no row, column or diagonal line should contain the same letter more than once. One horizontal line should spell the name correctly. What letter will replace the question mark?

SEE ANSWER 133

Paul wears Levi jeans, he travels on United Airlines and he thinks Anthony Hopkins is a great actor.

Does Paul drive a Porsche or a Jaguar?

SEE ANSWER 102

Turn the dials on this unusual safe to give
12 surnames of sports stars from the past and present.
(More than 8 is a good score.)

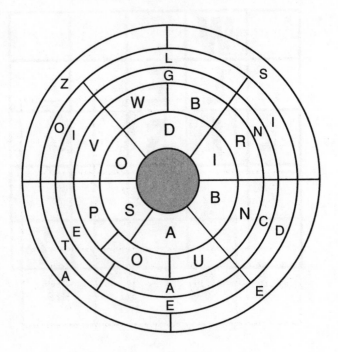

SEE ANSWER 114

Can you work out what letter needs to be inserted in the middle to form four sporting champions by combining opposite segments?

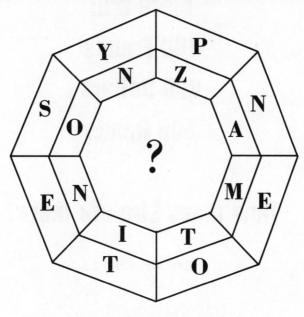

SEE ANSWER 123

Move from square to touching square – including diagonals – to discover the name of an order of monks.

E	N	I	C
E	D	E	T
J	N	I	B

SEE ANSWER 16

In a drawer at an international bank there are:

100 Francs

600 Dollars

500 Rands

How many Lira are there?

SEE ANSWER 24

The names of the following ten airlines can be found in this grid on vertical, horizontal and diagonal lines. Can you find them?

Aer Lingus
Aeroflot
Alitalia
Delta
Egypt Air
Finnair
Lufthansa
Monarch
Olympic
Swissair

O	B	X	R	C	Y	Y	K	H	A
L	L	G	I	R	X	T	B	E	P
Y	U	Z	A	I	G	O	R	P	F
M	F	C	T	A	T	L	E	D	H
P	T	Y	P	N	I	F	D	Z	C
I	H	Q	Y	N	V	O	M	W	R
C	A	K	G	I	X	R	F	K	A
B	N	U	E	F	D	E	K	V	N
H	S	W	I	S	S	A	I	R	O
Z	A	L	I	T	A	L	I	A	M

SEE ANSWER 34

Perfume manufacturers are bringing out new fragrances for the coming season.

Ralph Lauren has four new fragrances, Christian Dior has five and Givenchy has two new fragrances.

How many new scents will be promoted by Yves Saint Laurent?

SEE ANSWER 50

PUZZLE 163

The names of five authors are written here in code.
Who are they?

i) **TUFQIFO LJOH**
ii) **BHBUIB DISJTUJF**
iii) **KPIO HSJTIBN**
iv) **DIBSMFT EJDLFOT**
v) **HFPSHF PSXFMM**

SEE ANSWER 73

Some letters are missing from this alphabet. Rearrange the missing letters to form the name of a composer.

SEE ANSWER 8

PUZZLE 165

What letter should appear next in this series?

Z

X

U

Q

L

SEE ANSWER 91

Emma drinks Benedictine, she reads books by Sigmund Freud and holidays in Miami.

Is her hero Muhammad Ali or George Best?

SEE ANSWER 105

Turn the dials on this diagram to give 8 forenames and 8 family names of famous actors. Then match them up to give their full names. Who are they? (A score above 5 is very good.)

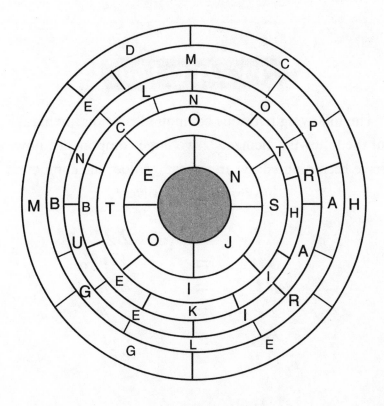

SEE ANSWER 117

There are eight floors in a high-rise block. The fifth floor has the only apartment with two bedrooms. Mrs Barber has a baby and cannot carry a buggy upstairs when the elevator is out of order. Mr and Mrs Elder also find climbing difficult now they are retired. Mr Archer likes the peace and quiet of living on the top floor. Mrs Cook and her daughter need a two-bedroom flat. Mr and Mrs Hooper live just below Mr Archer. Mrs Cook lives above Mr Gardener and below Mrs Driver. Mr and Mrs Fisher live above Mr and Mrs Elder.

Who lives where?

SEE ANSWER 97

PUZZLE 169

The following fictitious compound is primarily made up of the following elements. Two large components, however, have been omitted: what percentage does the compound have of gold and silver?

Al	=	22%
Sn	=	10%
Pt	=	8%
Fe	=	2%
Ag	=	??
Au	=	??

SEE ANSWER 178

If Henry drives a Mercedes, Tom drives a Honda, Sally drives a Mazda and Richard drives a Lincoln, what will car Brenda drive?

i)   Cadillac
ii)   Ford
iii)   Audi
iv)   Citroen
v)   Alfa
vi)   Triumph
vii)   Saab

SEE ANSWER 175

PUZZLE 171

Complete the square using the letters of T U R I N. When completed no row, column or diagonal line should contain the same letter more than once. One horizontal line should spell the city correctly. What letter will replace the question mark?

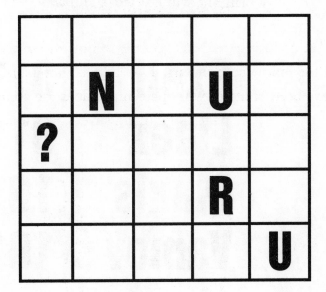

SEE ANSWER 172

PUZZLE 172

The serial numbers for these products all relate to their names?
What is the name of the last product?

NAME	SERIAL NO
HABBIZ	82249.62
EDDAN	5842.41
BACCAR	22361.81
?	94989.42

SEE ANSWER 177

PUZZLE 173

These four robots will only operate when the
correct code is programmed into their mainframes.
Which one will not work and why?

Exell   **0110**
Lidex   **0111**
Maxis   **1011**
Vamov   **1010**

SEE ANSWER 174

Rearrange these boxes in a 3 x 3 square in such a way that the adjoining letters are always the same. Then add the alphanumeric values of each line of three outer letters and convert back to letters to give the name of a Roman god.

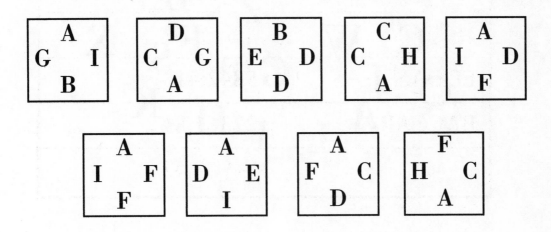

SEE ANSWER 171

The letters around each box and the one in the middle all have an American link. Which letters replace the question marks?

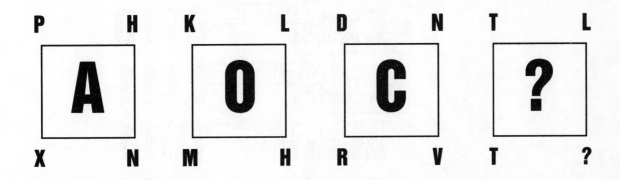

SEE ANSWER 179

PUZZLE 176

Some letters are missing from this alphabet. Rearrange the missing letters to form the name of a state in the USA.

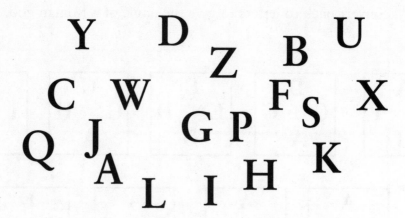

SEE ANSWER 3

PUZZLE 177

Here is a strange signpost to the burial grounds in Ancient Egypt.
How far is it to burial ground of Thoth?

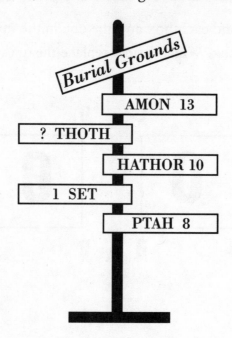

SEE ANSWER 169

Move from square to touching square – including diagonals – to discover the name of an actor.

S	T	W	O	O
A	T	C	I	O
E	L	N	L	D

SEE ANSWER 13

When manned space travel began, a piece of space material collected by cosmonauts contained a strange riddle.

Property of NEPTUNE

This is our NINTH expedition

A party of SEVEN astronauts

Setting up our IMPERIAL base

Over a period of FIFTY-ONE days

There followed a picture a dead US President.
Who was it?

(i) Adams (ii) Harrison (iii) Jackson (iv) Monroe (v) Van Buren

SEE ANSWER 176

PUZZLE 180

This is an unusual maze. Find four separate routes through it
without any route crossing another, although the paths may merge.
On each route collect 6 letters to give you four cities in the USA.

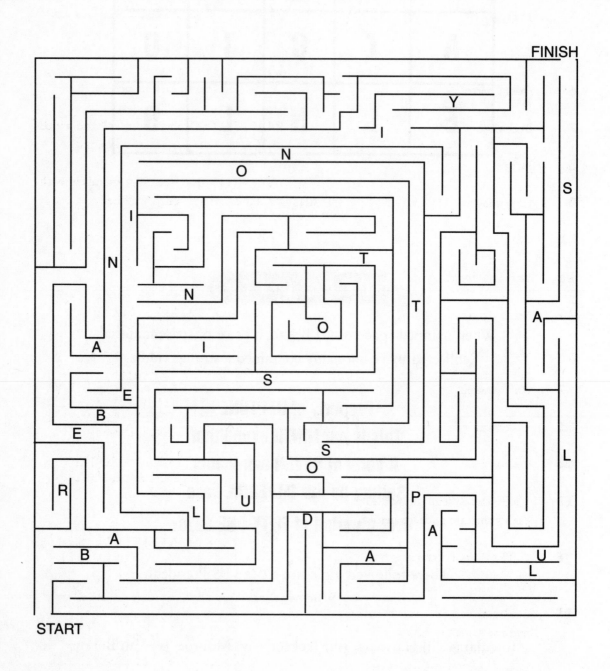

SEE ANSWER 159

1   Hawking.

2   Renault.

3   Vermont.

4   Yangtze.

5   Puebla.

6   Fidel Castro.

7   Bucharest.

8   Handel.

9   Copenhagen.

10   Tchaikovsky.

11   Sigmund Freud.

12   Pennsylvania.

13   Clint Eastwood.

14   Barbra Streisand.

15   Lamborghini.

16   Benedictine.

17   1003. The Roman numerals in each name are added together.

18   1. The Roman numerals in each are added together.

19   1.00 pm. The Roman numerals in each name are added together. A point is then placed two places in to give a time.

20   1. The Roman numerals in each drink give the amount.

21   1. The Roman numerals in each name are added together.

22   1050. The Roman numerals are added together in each place name.

23   50. The Roman numerals are added together in each name.

24   51. The Roman numerals are added together to give the amounts.

25   1106. The Roman numerals in each name are added together.

26   1551. The Roman numerals in each name are added together.

27

28

29

Y	N	J	Z	B	W	K	X	B	T	N	F	G
G	I	O	R	G	I	O	A	R	M	A	N	I
T	E	S	S	O	B	O	G	U	H	R	G	A
X	L	V	E	S	V	R	Y	C	R	N	B	N
R	K	Q	S	H	F	X	B	E	V	O	K	N
Z	N	G	S	W	L	J	D	O	Q	C	M	I
J	I	T	E	M	P	O	F	L	W	R	Q	V
Y	V	K	L	K	R	S	B	D	Z	E	S	E
W	L	N	L	D	B	H	P	F	Q	P	D	R
F	A	T	E	G	U	C	C	I	X	S	Y	S
X	C	A	L	T	P	Q	M	E	H	A	W	A
V	D	G	J	V	Z	D	Y	L	G	J	Z	C
S	T	U	S	S	Y	F	K	D	B	J	B	E

30

H	P	C	T	U	B	O	P	M	I
G	U	C	C	I	Q	K	F	N	J
M	B	K	W	T	M	I	G	T	C
J	N	P	A	C	O	E	Z	D	V
Q	X	V	D	A	R	S	X	Q	Y
Z	R	X	N	S	F	X	S	K	R
D	K	E	O	I	M	B	F	I	A
V	X	L	K	O	L	I	M	I	T
P	L	O	E	Y	Q	W	J	V	O
J	F	R	S	B	M	K	U	P	R

31

C	J	H	J	K	I	M	F	G	I	M	C	W
B	E	C	M	Z	K	Y	X	B	V	N	A	Y
J	R	I	A	O	S	J	V	H	A	Y	V	S
F	E	T	R	N	D	C	Y	V	N	D	O	E
K	M	S	C	H	E	P	H	E	L	K	K	L
G	Y	L	R	D	S	K	F	P	E	J	U	E
Z	B	E	O	X	U	E	G	A	N	M	S	S
C	A	A	S	W	K	W	B	T	D	D	A	A
P	T	H	S	R	G	M	W	C	L	Z	N	C
J	E	C	E	F	E	Y	V	A	Y	B	E	I
F	S	I	T	Y	R	Z	M	S	J	X	L	N
H	R	M	P	H	G	C	B	H	K	F	E	O
A	N	T	O	V	O	N	A	N	A	J	H	M

32

T	R	Y	J	P	Q	X	G	D	H	K	X
M	A	D	N	V	R	K	F	Z	F	W	Z
J	R	N	O	D	D	E	S	Y	J	O	T
P	S	N	O	T	A	R	E	H	S	Z	F
C	H	E	P	P	L	E	W	H	I	T	E
H	C	H	I	P	P	E	N	D	A	L	E
D	M	B	Y	Z	H	I	S	C	P	G	J
F	T	A	G	W	F	T	L	Y	I	B	M
X	U	K	D	D	U	O	D	L	N	T	X
M	V	C	P	A	C	K	L	W	I	G	K
K	W	G	R	K	M	O	V	R	U	H	Y
Z	H	T	R	X	W	W	B	N	Y	K	P

33

S	I	A	N	A	S	I	A	N	A	A
A	P	D	G	H	F	P	J	C	R	
F	C	E	G	I	R	A	M	A	A	
A	F	H	L	D	J	R	K	F	S	
R	Y	Q	U	L	Z	I	Z	R	M	
I	R	N	Z	X	B	S	F	X	A	
Q	E	V	K	W	O	O	Y	J	S	
B	H	K	V	D	W	C	U	G	I	
O	B	S	E	S	S	I	O	N	G	
R	O	I	D	S	S	I	M	C	D	

34

O	B	X	R	C	Y	Y	K	H	A
L	L	G	I	R	X	T	B	E	P
Y	U	Z	A	I	G	O	R	P	F
M	F	C	T	A	T	L	E	D	H
P	T	Y	P	N	I	F	D	Z	C
I	H	Q	Y	N	V	O	M	W	R
C	A	K	G	I	X	R	F	K	A
B	N	U	E	F	D	E	K	V	N
H	S	W	I	S	S	A	I	R	O
Z	A	L	I	T	A	L	I	A	M

35

W	Z	Q	E	P	R	V	H	E	F	M
T	O	U	S	Y	J	A	H	E	E	Z
T	N	S	I	G	K	L	U	L	S	W
I	I	E	U	F	H	K	G	E	E	P
P	C	A	R	H	X	I	H	C	E	H
D	A	N	C	H	B	L	G	U	L	J
A	P	P	M	S	Q	M	R	R	C	R
R	L	E	O	J	R	E	A	B	N	G
B	A	N	T	T	Z	R	N	P	H	Y
S	K	N	A	H	M	O	T	W	O	S
Y	R	B	X	F	Q	J	X	N	J	S

36

R	N	B	L	F	K	X	C	D	R
E	N	D	C	W	Q	H	S	O	E
N	E	G	A	W	S	K	L	O	V
A	O	H	J	K	O	L	B	P	O
U	R	G	V	D	S	F	Y	J	R
L	T	C	A	R	A	U	G	A	J
T	I	T	O	E	G	U	E	P	M
P	C	Y	T	O	Y	O	T	A	B
J	C	F	V	G	Z	C	W	D	K
E	K	D	P	M	H	Q	G	Y	F

37 Daniel, Exodus, Isaiah and Joshua can be found by pairing alternate segments.

38 Agassi, Becker, Hingis and Muster can be found by pairing adjacent segments.

39 Boston, Dallas, Denver and Newark can be found by pairing opposite segments.

40 Bogart, Heston, Marvin and Monroe can be found by pairing alternate segments.

41 Adagio, Presto, Sonata and Timbre can be found by pairing adjacent segments.

42 Darwin, Newton and Pascal can be found by pairing adjacent segments.

43 50. The number of letters in each name, multiplied by 10, gives the amount.

44 9. The alphabetical position of the last letter of the name gives the amount.

45 7. The consonants in each name gives the number of recipes.

46 8. Each vowel is given a value of one and each consonant is give a value of two. These are added together in each name to give the amount.

47 13. The alphanumeric values of the letters in each champagne are added together. The total is divided by 10 to give the price.

48 22. In each name a vowel is given a value of five and a consonant is given a value of three. These are added together to give the amount.

49 3. The alphabetical position of the first letter gives the amount.

50 Six. The number of vowels in each name give the amount.

51 340. Each vowel is given a value of 30 and each consonant is given a value of 50. These are added together in each city name to give the distance.

52 Budapest
London
Stockholm
Madrid

53 Pennsylvania
Massachusetts
Connecticut
Minnesota

54 Nixon
Reagan
Clinton
Truman

55 Dustin Hoffman
Steve Martin
Patrick Swayze
Melanie Griffiths

56 Annie Lennox
Janet Jackson
Mariah Carey
Kylie Minogue

57   Handel
Beethoven
Vivaldi
Mozart

58   Brooklyn because it is a city, the others are states (Florida, Delaware and Arizona).

59   Spielberg. The others are scientists: Archimedes, Galileo and Einstein.

60   Gandhi
Castro
Churchill
Reagan

61   Gunnell
Backley
Johnson

62   Travolta
Stallone
Goldberg

63   Pizzicato
Crescendo
Larghetto

64   Nicaragua
Maracaibo
Tanganyka

65   Dudley Moore and Eddie Murphy.

66   (The alphabet is 6 letters out of phase)
    i)   Pat Cash
    ii)   Steffi Graf
    iii)   Andre Agassi
    iv)   Martina Navratilova
    v)   Conchita Martinez

67   i)   Bill Clinton
    ii)   Abraham Lincoln
    iii)   George Washington
    iv)   Harry S. Truman
    v)   John F. Kennedy
    vi)   Ulysses Grant

68   i)   Minnesota
    ii)   Texas
    iii)   Alaska
    iv)   California
    v)   Florida
    vi)   Louisiana

69   i)   Odin
    ii)   Hermes
    iii)   Osiris
    iv)   Poseidon
    v)   Athena
    vi)   Cupid

70   i)   Einstein
    ii)   Celsius
    iii)   Newton
    iv)   Copernicus
    v)   Pascal
    vi)   Darwin

71   i)   Roberto Baggio
    ii)   Dennis Bergkamp
    iii)   Kevin Keegan
    iv)   Eric Cantona
    v)   Jurgen Klinsmann

72   i)   Queen
    ii)   Simply Red
    iii)   Bon Jovi
    iv)   Genesis
    v)   Simple Minds

73
   i)   Stephen King
   ii)   Agatha Christie
   iii) John Grisham
   iv) Charles Dickens
   v)   George Orwell

74
   i)   Yul Brynner
   ii)   Cary Grant
   iii) Clark Gable
   iv) Keanu Reaves
   v)   Tony Curtis

75   Bob Marley.

76   Michael Chang.

77   Gail Devers.

78   Mel Gibson.

79   Liz McColgan.

80   Chicago.

81   O and N. They all are scientists: Newton, Young, Edison, Rontgen

82   O and N. The stars are: Collins, Lennon, Jones, Diamond and Jackson.

83   A and O. These are all musical terms: Opera, Adagio, Aria, Largo, Rubato and Sonata.

84   Q. The alphabet is moved five letters, then four, then three, etc.

85   T and V. The alphabet with the following sequence of spaces between the letters: two, three, two, four, two, five and two.

86   W. The letters are in alphabetical sequence, no straight lines, one straight line etc.)

87   D and F. On a Qwerty keyboard, these are the first letters, reading from the left, of the middle row.

88   P. They are the initials of the planets: Mercury, Venus, Earth, Mars, Jupiter, Saturn, Uranus, Neptune and Pluto.

89   Z. Each letter is one alphabetical place after the number.

90   L. The letters are those which only contain straight lines

91   F. The letters are the alphabet in reverse, firstly missing one letter, then two, then three etc.

92   X and B. Every fourth letter of the alphabet forms one series and every fifth letter from the end of the alphabet forms the other series. These are merged together.

93   Finishing order is 12, 3, 11, 21, 7 and 8 last.

94

Mr Evans	Mrs Graves	Mrs Davis	Mr Adams
Mrs Harris	Mrs Bates	Mr Francis	Mr Conners

95   Andrew on Sunshine Boy wins the race, Marc on Blue Moon comes second, John on Silver Shadow is third and Dan on Redwing finishes last.

96 Charlie leaves at the 1st floor.
Barbie leaves at the 2nd floor.
Debbie leaves at the 3rd floor.
Angie leaves at the 4th floor.
Frankie leaves at the 5th floor.
Eddie leaves at the 6th floor.

97 8th floor – Mr Archer
7th floor – Mr and Mrs Hooper
6th floor – Mrs Driver
5th floor – Mrs Cook and daughter
4th floor – Mr Gardener
3rd floor – Mr and Mrs Fisher
2nd floor – Mr and Mrs Elder
1st floor – Mrs Baker

98 Monarch. The first letters placed together give the name of Adam.

99 Martina Navratilova. The last letters placed together give the name Laura.

100 Tyson. The third letters placed together give the name Louis.

101 McEnroe. The first letter of the first word gives the first letter of Jean. The second letter of the second word gives the second letter of Jean and so on.

102 Porsche. The first letters, when placed together in reverse order, give the name Paul.

103 Laurent Perrier. The last letters, when placed together in reverse order, give the name Rolfe.

104 Coco. The last letters, when placed in reverse order, read Olga.

105 Muhammad Ali. The fourth letters when placed together read Emma.

106 A. Jurgen Lehl. The last letter of the last word gives the first of Lena, the penultimate letter of the penultimate word gives the second of Lena, and so on.

107 Peugeot. The penultimate letters in each car name give Theo.

108 Each of the four names contains the name of Chinese Dynasty. They are: Wei, Chin, Han and Tang.

109 (i)   Add Joel to get John Lennon.
(ii)   Add Job to get Bon Jovi.
(iii)   Add Amos to get Alison Moyet.

110 Lira

I	L	L	I	N	O	I	S
M	I	C	H	I	G	A	N
A	R	K	A	N	S	A	S
M	A	R	Y	L	A	N	D

111 Tony Curtis.

C	O	P	P	E	R
M	U	R	P	H	Y
M	A	R	V	I	N
M	A	R	T	I	N
G	A	R	C	I	A
R	E	E	V	E	S

112 Tenor.

P	I	T	C	H
O	P	E	R	A
L	E	N	T	O
C	H	O	R	D
L	A	R	G	O

113 Lancia.

B	I	L	L	Y
B	R	I	A	N
D	I	A	N	A
B	R	U	C	E
M	A	R	I	E
S	A	R	A	H

114 Spitz, Borg, Bowe, Lewis, Ali, Pele, Zico, Senna, Lauda, Bats, David, Coe.

115 Holly Hunter, Sally Field, Daryl Hannah, Meg Ryan, Demi Moore, Winona Ryder, Jane Fonda, Bette Davis.

116 Huron, Erie, Apal, Baykal, Cha, Onega, Eyre, Erne, Neagh, Volta, Geneva.

117 Tom Hanks, John Cleese, Tom Cruise, Brad Pitt, Bob Hope, Mel Gibson, Al Pacino, Hugh Grant.

118 Alto, Bass, Chord, Largo, Lento, Opera, Opus, Presto, Rondo, Rubato, Sonato, Tempo, Tenor.

119 E. Elgar
Bizet
Grieg
Verdi

120 O. Cairo
Hanoi
Seoul
Tokyo

121 N. Hymen
Venus
Diana
Woden

122 A. Tango
Polka
Rumba
Samba

123 S. Tyson
Spitz
Senna
Moses

124 A. Indi,
China
Delta
Pan Am

125 N. Monet
Rodin
Munch
Ernst

126 P.

P	A	R	I	S
I	S	P	A	R
A	R	I	S	**P**
S	P	A	R	I
R	I	S	P	A

128 Y.

B	R	Y	A	N
A	N	B	R	Y
R	Y	A	N	B
N	B	R	Y	A
Y	A	N	B	R

127 I.

I	D	A	H	O
H	O	I	D	A
D	A	H	O	I
O	I	D	A	H
A	H	O	I	D

129 S.

X	A	S	T	E
S	T	E	X	A
E	X	A	S	T
A	S	T	E	X
T	E	X	A	**S**

130 M.

A	L	M	P	S
M	P	S	A	L
S	A	L	M	P
L	M	P	S	A
P	S	A	L	M

132 L.

L	O	T	U	S
T	U	S	L	O
S	L	O	T	U
O	T	U	S	L
U	S	L	O	T

131 F.

U	D	F	R	E
F	R	E	U	D
E	U	D	F	R
D	F	R	E	U
R	E	U	D	F

133 W.

E	W	I	S	L
S	L	E	W	I
W	I	S	L	E
L	E	W	I	S
I	S	L	E	W

134 Maryland.

135 Winnipeg.

136 Brad Pitt.

137 Jeremiah.

138 Portland.

139 Meatloaf.

140 J. The vowels have been omitted from the surnames and the initial of the first name is in the middle of the box: Tom Cruise, Johnny Depp, Gary Cooper and John Wayne.

141

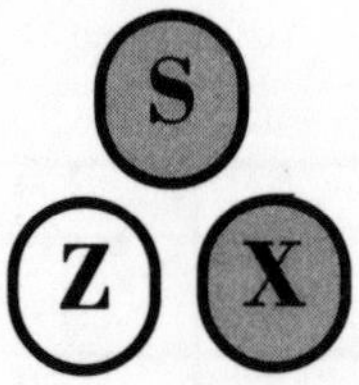

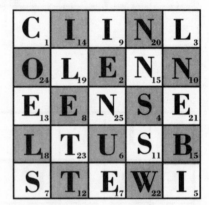

142 T. The cities, without vowels and the initial of the states they are in. Orlando (Florida), Detroit (Michigan), Denver (Colorado) and Dallas (Texas).

143 O. The middle letter of each name is in the middle of the box. Fonda, Hanks, Wayne and Stone.

144 A. The letters outside are consonants of famous tennis players. They are: (top) Borg and Graf, (bottom) Agassi and Cash. The letters inside the triangles are the initials of their nationality. They are Swedish, German, American and Australian respectively.

145 Malaysia and Hong Kong.

146 Chopin and Handel.

147 Exodus and Joshua.

148 Virginia and Delaware,

149 (Calvin) Coolidge and (James) Buchanan.

150 The scientists are: Celsius, Einstein, Bell, Newton.

C 1	I 14	I 9	N 20	L 3
O 24	L 19	E 2	N 15	N 10
E 13	E 8	N 25	S 4	E 21
L 18	T 23	U 6	S 11	B 15
S 7	T 12	E 17	W 22	I 5

151 The cartoon characters are: Bambi, Cinderella, Pluto and Yogi.

I 24	R 11	P 16	I 5	O 22
B 1	C 6	G 23	E 10	A 15
E 12	L 17		Y 21	B 4
I 7	A 2	T 19	L 14	D 9
U 18	L 13	N 8	M 3	O 20

152 The great writers are: Stephen King, Oscar Wilde, William Shakespeare and Jane Austen.

A₂₇	E₆	W₁₇	N₄₂	S₂₉	K₈	L₁₉
R₁₆	N₄₉	M₂₈	N₇	I₁₈	E₄₃	H₃₀
H₅	I₂₆	A₄₁	R₃₈	P₃₅	D₂₀	I₉
E₄₈	A₁₅	E₃₆	S₁	J₄₀	A₃₁	A₄₄
L₂₅	P₄	E₃₉	S₃₄	N₃₇	N₁₀	E₂₁
C₁₄	T₄₇	T₂	I₂₃	O₁₂	U₄₅	K₃₂
E₃	L₂₄	S₁₃	S₄₆	E₃₃	W₂₂	G₁₁

153 The stars are: Tom Cruise, Mel Gibson, Robert De Niro, Steve Martin, Whoopi Goldberg, and Jane Fonda.

O₄₅	T₃₂	E₁₁	S₁₆	I₄₇	O₃₀	T₁	I₁₄
M₁₀	O₁₇	P₄₆	S₃₁	L₁₂	B₁₅	G₄₈	R₂₉
E₃₃	O₄₄	G₅₅	N₅₈	D₅₁	N₆₂	G₁₃	O₂
N₁₈	E₉	B₅₂	O₆₁	R₅₄	A₅₇	I₂₈	O₄₉
H₄₃	V₃₄	E₅₉	J₅₆	D₆₃	L₅₀	M₃	T₂₄
S₈	R₁₉	A₆₄	E₅₃	F₆₀	D₂₅	R₃₈	N₂₇
E₃₅	W₄₂	B₂₁	U₆	A₃₇	I₄₀	R₂₃	C₄
O₂₀	I₇	M₃₆	N₄₁	E₂₂	R₅	E₂₆	T₃₉

154 The books are: Samuel, Joshua, Mathew, Isaiah, Daniel and Esther.

L₃₀	N₂₇	H₁₀	A₂₃	R₃₆	D₂₅
U₁₁	I₂₂	E₂₉	A₂₆	S₉	S₂₀
I₂₈	E₃₁	O₈	A₂₁	H₂₄	E₃₅
J₇	A₁₂	E₅	A₂	I₁₉	D₁₆
S₃₂	S₁	X₁₄	U₁₇	H₃₄	M₃
E₁₃	L₆	T₃₃	U₄	O₁₅	S₁₈

155 The golfers are: Arnold Palmer, Nick Faldo, Tom Watson, Nick Pice and Gary Player.

O₂₃	P₄₄	C₃₃	A₈	O₂₁	R₄₂	N₃₁
K₃₄	A₁	T₂₂	Y₄₃	I₃₂	P₇	D₂₀
L₄₅	M₂₄	L₉	R₁₂	C₁₅	N₃₀	A₄₁
R₂	P₃₅	I₁₄	Y₄₇	M₁₀	L₁₉	D₆
W₂₅	A₄₆	E₁₁	K₁₆	N₁₃	G₄₀	O₂₉
R₃₆	N₃	E₄₈	T₂₇	C₃₈	L₅	A₁₈
R₄₉	A₂₆	I₃₇	O₄	F₁₇	S₂₈	E₃₉

156 Malachi
Genesis
Numbers
Ezekiel
The last letter of two
of the four names is
the same.

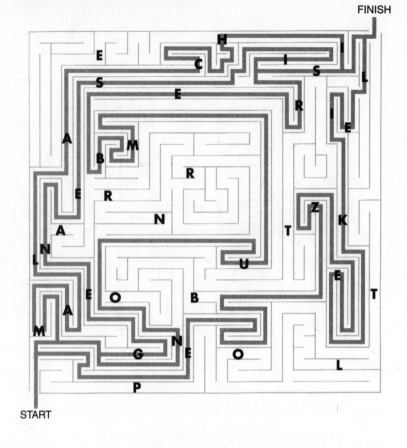

157 Turner
Kilmer
Taylor
Gibson
The first letter of two of
the routes is the same,
and the last letter of
three of the routes is
the same.

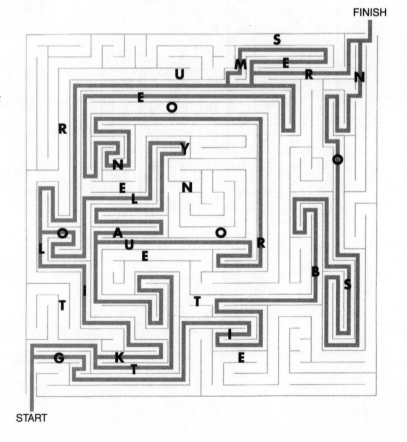

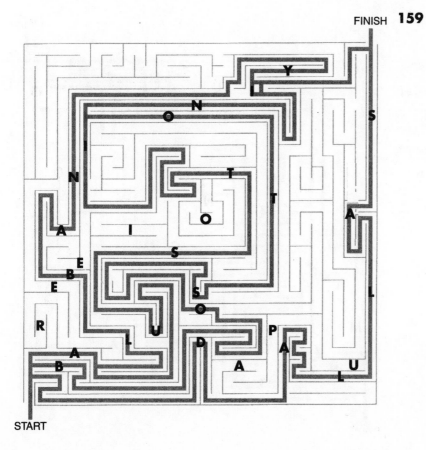

FINISH

158
Rococo
Rubato
Sonata
Timbre
The first letter of two of the routes is the same and the last letter of two of the routes is the same.

START

FINISH **159**
Albany
Austin
Dallas
Boston
The first letter of two of the routes is the same and the last letter of two of the routes is the same.

START

FINISH

160 Gunnell
Freeman
Johnson
Zelezny
The last letter of two of
the routes is the same.

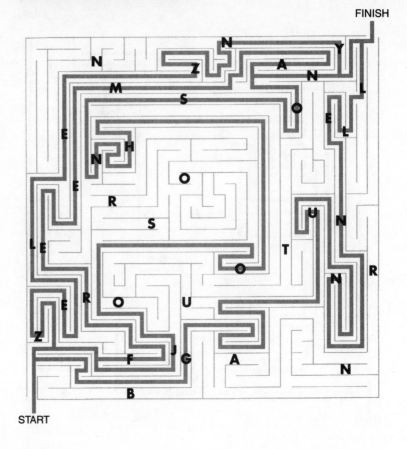

START

161 Edison
Darwin
Euclid
Pascal
The first letter of two of
the routes is the same
and the last letter of two
of the routes is the same.

FINISH

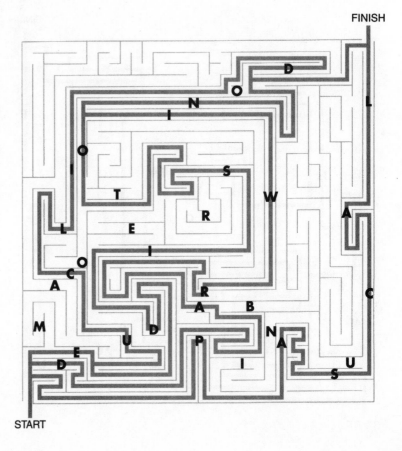

START

162 1st and 5th – their final position is based on the number of vowels in their names.

163 4th. The finishing order was: 1st, Ferrari; 2nd, Audi; 3rd, Renault; 4th, Ligier, 5th, Mercedes.

164 Bunny was for Dairy, Ermintrude was for Beef and Wilma was for Beef. Take the each name's initial letters' alphanumeric value; even = dairy, odd = beef.

165 Each value is the sum of Roman numerals in the person's name: Brenda had 500, Axel had 60, Norman had 1000 and Charlie had 151.

166 Mr Becker follows Mr Lewis and then Mr Fischer and then Mr Schultz. The order is based on number of consonants in each person's name.

167 The second letter of the drink is the first letter of each person's name:
Tia Maria for Ian
Vodka for Olga
Whiskey for Harry
Rum for Ursula.

168 The third letter from the end of the car name is the beginning letter of the person's name.
Toyota belongs to Oliver
Rover to Vera
Jaguar to Ursula
Fiat to Irene
Honda to Nigel.

169 12. The number of letters between the alphanumeric position of the first and last letters of each name.

170 Queen Anne. The number of spaces in the alphabet between the second and third letters of each person's name.

171 Zeus.

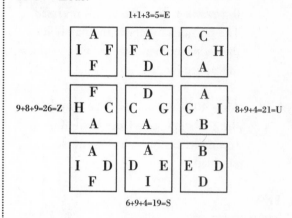

172 U.

173 Monroe. The penultimate letter of each name is the same.

174 Lidex. The numbers are the value of the roman numerals contained in the other names added together. Lidex should be 561.

175 Triumph. The second letter of the driver and the manfacturer of the car are the same.

ANSWERS

176 Van Buren. Neptune was spelled out in the capitalized words of the succeeding lines of the riddle.

177 IBIDIX. The alphanumeric value of the last number, after the dot, is reversed. The previous numbers alternately have their alphanumeric values or the values multiplied by 2.

178 Au = 40%, Ag = 12%. The difference in the alphanumeric values of the first and second letters of each element is doubled.

179

The letters read clockwise from the top left are the consonants in the state capitals and the state's initial is in the middle. Phoenix in Arizona, Oklahoma (City) in Oklahoma, Denver in Colorado and Atlanta in Georgia.

180 Carter
Eisenhower
Johnson
Reagan
Roosevelt

IDENTITY CRISIS

Your name is Christian Alexander Washington.